The History of Rotherwas Munitions Factory, Hereford

The History of Rotherwas Munitions Factory, Hereford

by
John Edmonds

LOGASTON PRESS
The Holme, Church Road,
Eardisley, Herefordshire HR3 6NJ

First published by Logaston Press 2004
Reprinted 2017, 2018
Copyright © text: John Edmonds
Copyright © illustrations as per credits
(recent uncredited photographs are the author's property)

All rights reserved. No part of this publication may be reproduced, stored in a retrieval system,
or transmitted, in any form or by any means, electronic, mechanical, photocopying, recording
or otherwise, without prior permission

ISBN 978 1 904396 27 7

Typeset by Logaston Press
and printed in Great Britain by Bell & Bain Ltd, Glasgow

Logaston Press is committed to a sustainable future for our business,
our readers and our planet. The book in your hands is made from paper
certified by the Forest Stewardship Council.

Cover illustration: *A view of several of the enclosures in the Northern Section formed by cast-in-situ concrete blast walls which surrounded the wooden working buildings of the Second World War (Andrew Terry, Herefordshire Council)*

Those working in the National Factories during the First World War did at least receive a Certificate of Service when their employment was ended after the armistice of November 1918. Workers in the Royal Ordnance Filling Factories who were told to seek work elsewhere at the end of the Second World War were not given any form of official recognition nor has any been forthcoming ever since.

The work of those filling munitions was vital to the winning of the wars. The work they did was boring in the extreme, hard and dangerous. It demanded total concentration if mistakes were to be avoided. Much of the explanation as to why we won both wars can be said to be due to the superior way that industry was mobilised.

This book is dedicated to those who worked in munitions between 1914 and 1918 and between 1932 and 1945.

Contents

		page
	Acknowledgments	viii
	Foreword by Barrie Trinder	xi
1	The Background	1
2	The Early History of the Site	9
3	The Filling Operation during the First World War	21
4	Labour in the First World War	35
5	November 1918 to September 1939	47
6	Chemical Warfare from 1918 onwards	53
7	Rotherwas at War – 1939 to 1945	59
8	Wartime Accommodation Development in Hereford	79
9	The Change to Civilian Use	83
	Endnotes	103
	Index	111

Acknowledgments

This book is based on the research undertaken during two years work leading to a Masters Degree at the University of Birmingham. It was Dr. Barrie Trinder, my academic supervisor there, who first set my interest alight in the subject of Industrial Archaeology during a previous Certificate of Higher Education, two year course. He was guide, mentor and friend during the two years of study for the Masters Degree and has been kind enough to write an introduction to this book.

Four fellow students from the CHE course often held the end of a tape measure for me during the times we surveyed various buildings at Rotherwas. The help and comments of Dr. Mike Harrison, his wife Ann, Brian Malaws and Tony Parkes have been most valuable.

Steve Macklin of Bishopthorpe most generously gave me a number of maps I have not found elsewhere which he had obtained when doing a project on Rotherwas. Andrew Terry, Estates Officer for Herefordshire Council, who looks after the Rotherwas Industrial Estate, first took me round the site and later was generous with his time in helping me to track down maps and other paperwork. His photographs have been most valuable and we have used several. Gerry Stokes of Halcrow plc produced a report for Hereford and Worcester Council and he gave me a copy together with a number of aerial photographs. Mike Christenson of the World War Two Railway Study Group was most helpful with advice and documents and he provided details of the railway layout at Rotherwas. Dave Chatfield replied to a letter of mine in the *Hereford Times* asking for information about Rotherwas. He and a colleague had begun to research the history of the site in the early 90s. He gave me all the information they had uncovered together with a number of plans of the 1930s reconstruction. Eric Gittoes of Arctic Gold, a company based at Rotherwas showed me a copy of the German 1940 Luftwaffe reconnaissance photograph of Rotherwas. Neil Hirst gave me a copy of his unpublished *50 years of A Lighting Company in Hereford* which provided information about the central section in the post war years.

Sue Hubbard, now retired from the Hereford Record Office, and Robin Hill, Head Librarian at Hereford City, and their staffs have been helpful in suggesting lines of inquiry as well as providing the vast number of documents I requested to see. In particular I must compliment whichever inspired member of staff at the Record Office catalogued the Minutes of the Hereford Deanery Committee under the heading: munitions. I would otherwise never have thought of looking at these but they produced a marvellous picture of the moralistic, middle class attitude displayed by the city and its inhabitants at the arrival of the work people engaged in the filling operation in both wars.

I have nothing but praise for the efficiency of the staff at the Public Records Office of the National Archives at Kew. I made extensive use of their on-line catalogue Procat, allowing me to narrow down my search before spending several days working there.

But above all else I have been privileged to be able to talk to a number of those who worked at Rotherwas during its time as a Royal Ordnance Factory and to their relatives who shared memories with me. None of the workpeople were younger than 75 and Mrs. Carmichael was 96 when I talked to her. She started work as a process worker on the Northern Section in 1936 and by 1946, when she left, she was a forewomen and I am sure, a formidable one at that. Dave Chatfield also interviewed a group of people including another 96-year-old, Mrs. Winifred Thompson, the only contact with anyone who worked there in the First World War. She was there from 1916 to 1918 eventually becoming the overseer for Filling House No. 13 on the Northern Section. Others I talked to include Mrs. Doris Evans who worked in Unit 3 of the Southern Section; Mrs. Winifred Field, an Examiner of Warlike Stores for approximately 18 months from July 1940; Mrs. Gittings, first working in the Northern Section and then as a Process Worker filling 25 pounder shells on the Southern Section from 1940 to 1946; Mrs. Eileen Godding whose mother-in-law, a nurse in the welfare department, and her sister-in-law both worked at Rotherwas – both lived in Wormbridge and travelled to work by bus; Mrs. Peggy Jones who worked as a checker hand stemming bombs on the Southern Section from 1940 to 1943; Mrs. Hughes and Mrs. Lewis, sisters whose father was senior electrician at the factory coming from Woolwich to take the position – they lived in one of the cottages near to the site of Rotherwas House; Mr. Gordon Morris of Leominster whose mother and uncle both worked at Rotherwas, his uncle being one of those killed in the bombing raid of 1942; Mrs. Sally Price who worked at Rotherwas from 1942 onwards and lived in the Red Hill Hostel; Mrs. Margaret Smith whose mother, father and aunt all worked at Rotherwas – her mother was killed in the bombing raid of July 1942 and her father was awarded a medal for bravery during it; Mrs. Phyllis Taylor who was employed at Rotherwas from July 1940 to September 1945 first as an Examiner of Warlike Stores and then as an Overlooker; Mr. Brian Thomas who wrote to tell me that his father worked as an inspector at Rotherwas from 1938 until the 1944 explosion when he was transferred to Kirby Royal Ordnance Factory in Lancashire; Mr. Mike Wilkinson whose father and mother both worked at Rotherwas; Mr. Gordon Wood whose uncle was senior shunter for the GWR at Rotherwas. It was Gordon Wood who told me about the honest boxes for the railway staff which allowed me to find the one example left on the site.

These people were rightly proud of what they or their relatives had done. Those who worked there felt at the time, and still do now, that what they did played an important part in winning the war. Mrs. Carmichael perhaps summed it up. 'I wasn't liked as forewoman', she told me. 'I wouldn't let the girls get away with anything. I wasn't going to let our boys have shells that didn't work.'

Working with Andy Johnson my editor, should perhaps be likened to being cross-examined in court. But thank you Andy, the book is much improved by your efforts. He found many errors but those which remain are down to me.

Finally but never least, there is my partner Els Wilms. I cannot thank her enough for her support. Without it I am sure I would never have obtained my degree, much less have written this book. Thanks Els. You may have the kitchen table back at least until the next time.

Introduction

Archaeology, the study of the physical remains of the past, whether artefacts, images, earthworks or standing structures, is as relevant to our understanding of 20th-century Britain as it is to our knowledge of the Middle Ages or classical Greece. We may admire the elegance of some aspects of the 20th century, the design of some motor cars and locomotives, the scale of some suspension bridges, the clean logical lines of some Modernist buildings, just as we may be repelled by some shopping centres or tower block estates. We can gain understanding both from favourable and hostile reactions. Some aspects of 20th-century archaeology are well-preserved. Artefacts of many kinds, aircraft, motor vehicles, railway locomotives are displayed in national museums and are lovingly conserved by enthusiasts. It is relatively easy to study some aspects of the archaeology of the two world wars of the 20th century, from Spitfires and Matilda tanks to ration books and gas masks, that are displayed in many locally-managed museums as well as at such places as Duxford, Cosford and Bovington.

Yet there is much about the archaeology of the two world wars, and about the history of 20th-century Britain generally, that is difficult to unravel. In both wars many changes in the landscape took place under the authority of direct orders from central government, and under an umbrella of censorship. While most such actions were duly recorded, it is often difficult to trace the documentation, and to add to the official record the testimonies of those who saw and experienced what was happening. Wartime was a time of dispersal, and those responsible for changes in one place subsequently moved elsewhere. Recent studies of the remains of the defences built under the threat of invasion in 1940-41 have shown that very little information about such matters was previously available in the published literature.

While many historians have acknowledged the importance of the National Factories, set up by the Ministry of Munitions in the First World War, and the Royal Ordnance Factories of the Second World War, there have been few detailed studies of individual munitions works, and scarcely any that cover their full histories, from the acquisition of the sites by government to the present time. The factory at Rotherwas on the southern edge of Hereford is unusual in that, having been built during the First World War, it was retained in government ownership during the 1920s and '30s, to be revived during the rearmament programme that preceded the outbreak of hostilities with Germany in 1939. Many of the other munitions works built between 1915 and 1918 were abandoned. The factory at Banbury, for example, has since the early 1920s been no more that a range of substantial earthworks, grazed, not always safely, by cattle, and now bordered by the M40 motorway.

John Edmonds's study of the munitions factory at Rotherwas is important in several contexts. It contributes substantially to our understanding of the munitions industry generally, and is a valuable supplement to the long-term view of the industry provided by English Heritage in Wayne Cocroft's *Dangerous Energy*

xi

(2000). It is more specifically an addition to what we know about the manufacture of munitions in the two world wars, providing much enlightenment on topics that the writers of the official histories were unable to discuss. It raises pertinent questions about the manufacture of gas projectiles, and their role in the final stages of the First World War, and even about the use of such weapons in the 1920s.

The significance of the book is not confined to those aspects that are directly connected with military history. The Rotherwas factory exemplifies many social changes of the 20th century. John Edmonds shows that it profoundly changed some aspects of the city of Hereford, a community of modest size, which in 1914, apart from the factory-based manufacture of cider that had developed in the late 19th century, had only the limited range of small-scale industries, corn mills, maltings, tanneries and agricultural engineering works, that could be found in most market towns. Much of the city's living was gained through its role as the centre of county and diocesan administration. The impact of large numbers of incoming female workers aroused astonishing even bizarre reactions from some pillars of the local community. John Edmonds shows something of the implications of government direction of labour on those who were most affected. The munitions factory totally changed the landscape of the southern outskirts of Hereford, and in the Second World War also stimulated the building of flat-roofed houses, similar to those that can be seen around Swynnerton, Featherstone and other Royal Ordnance Factories. The lasting economic significance of the munitions works was that it led to the creation of an industrial zone alongside the River Wye that was the principal focus of economic growth in the region in the second half of the 20th century, and appears likely to remain so in the foreseeable future.

John Edmonds has used a commendably wide range of sources in his research. The Public Record Office (now the National Archive) has performed a great service to historians by making much of its catalogue available on line, and through that catalogue it has been possible to track down sources, some in the most unpromising files, that have provided the foundation for a thoroughly authoritative history of the factory. Local sources have also been used with skill and imagination. To read the Hereford newspapers was an obvious research task, but it was hardly to be expected that the records of the diocese would prove such a fruitful source of information on the social history of the factory. Much use has been made of visual sources, ranging from Ruskin Spear's painting of the devastation caused by the explosion at the factory in May 1944, to aerial photographs taken both by the RAF. John Edmonds has also made considerable use of the recollections of those who worked at the factory, and has used their understandably sharp memories of days of disaster to tease out information about the day-to-day routine of munitions manufacture. Above all this is an archaeological study, in which the author continually poses and re-poses questions relating what is known from documents, photographs or recollections to what remains to be seen on the ground.

The archaeological legacy of the munitions factory has diminished and will continue to diminish as buildings are adapted to the needs of the 21st century, whether these are wartime huts now used for manufacturing or storage on the industrial estate or houses whose window frames or flat roofs require replacement.

John Edmonds's achievement has been to provide a record of what remains of the Rotherwas factory in the opening years of the 21st century, and to explain the great outline and much of the significant detail of its history. Other documentary sources may come to light in future years. The publication of this book may awaken the memories of people who worked at the factory who now live many miles from Hereford, and they may have significant information to contribute to the story. Earthmoving and demolition during the redevelopment of the site may uncover fresh archaeological evidence. This study will provide a setting into which such new evidence can be placed. It is, in that respect, a major contribution to the history of Hereford and Herefordshire. It also illuminates the manufacture of munitions, the role of government in industry, the changing roles of women in society, and many other aspects of the broader history of Britain during the 20th century.

Barrie Trinder
Shrewsbury, September 2004

1 The Background

In August 1914 the 120,000 strong British Expeditionary Force[1] had helped to stem the German advance at the start of the First World War, but only at the cost of heavy casualties. It was not long before the armies began to dig in and within a matter of weeks trenches stretched some 450 miles from the Channel coast to the Swiss frontier. The stalemate that was trench warfare had arrived. For the next three and half years, until the German advances in the spring of 1918, each side desperately tried to break through the enemy's defences into the open ground behind them. Terrain was won and lost, but essentially the fighting took place in a band little more than 40 miles wide. Withdraw but ten miles from this band and life went on as normal: fields were tilled, crops harvested, people went to church and lived a relatively normal life. Within the area fought over, guns pounded bricks and mortar to dust, men dug trenches ever deeper, unwound endless miles of barbed wire and planned defences where machine gun bullets made advance all but certain death.

Over the course of the war artillery developed apace. That which the British Expeditionary Force took to France at the beginning of the conflict was woefully inadequate for the trench war that developed – the guns too light and the shells often misfiring or failing to explode at all. Yet artillery was to account for more deaths than the machine gun. Estimates vary, but between 70 and 80% of the casualties on the western front were caused by artillery shells. As early as November 1914 *The Times* reported 'Trenches and always trenches, and within range of the concealed guns invisibility the supreme law ... Day after day the butchery of the unknown by the unseen'.[2] Of the near 900,000 fatalities among British and Empire troops in France almost a half have no known grave, the result of either being blown to pieces or buried in the debris of a bombardment.

In August 1914 the British Expeditionary Force had taken 486 artillery pieces to France, a total that had risen to 6,709 in use by the middle of 1918. (The munitions industry actually manufactured 25,031 guns in the period.) British guns fired 170,385,295 rounds during the war, a total which included 4,283,550 shells used before the attack on Passchendaele between 17 and 30 July 1917. The most concentrated barrage was that preceding the attack on the Hindenberg Line when 943,847 rounds were fired in the 24 hours from noon on 28 September 1918.[3] But it was not just the size and number of guns that changed – so too had their precision and accuracy.

In *The Great War and the Shaping of the Twentieth Century,* Winter and Bagget state that it was at the Battle of Passchendaele in 1917 that assault by artillery finally became a science,[4] and by the summer of 1918 that artillery had developed into a war-winning force. Improvements in the guns themselves allowed them to fire heavier shells that penetrated more deeply before exploding. The ability to range the guns accurately through the use of sound detectors, precise mapping and aerial observation led to the introduction of a short but much more effective bombardment immediately before an attack – not fully developed at the time of Passchendaele but a most important part of the assault on the Hindenberg Line. The short bombardment reintroduced an all important measure of surprise, allowing the infantry to attack before the enemy was able to bring up reserves.

This increase in firepower demanded a vast increase in the supply of munitions. In May 1915 reports in the *Times* and the *Daily Mail* that an attack by the British at Artois had failed because of a shortage of shells, led to the appointment of the then Chancellor of the Exchequer, Lloyd George, to head a new Ministry of Munitions. He spent a year in the post before replacing Asquith as Prime Minister, a year which has been said to have revolutionised British industry.[5] During it the Ministry oversaw the development of more than 200 new factories, many in areas where no industrial activity had ever previously been undertaken.[6] In 1917 Churchill became Minister of Munitions. In 1918 he was planning for a mobile war in 1919 in which troops would be moved by lorry and the Ministry bought 650 acres of land at Slough where they began to build stocks of motorised vehicles. This site became the Slough Trading Estate.

The munitions industry employed huge numbers of people and by developing new systems and working practices dramatically increased productivity. During the war new management structures for munitions factories were utilized almost on an *ad hoc* basis to suit the requirements of a particular area. Where available, local businessmen were brought in to build and run factories that were funded from central funds.[7] In other cases, as with the National Filling Factory at Rotherwas, the design and construction of the factory was controlled by His Majesty's Office of Works with production then becoming the responsibility of the Ministry of Munitions.

The 5th Australian siege battery in 1917 on the Ypres-Comines canal sometime during the Third Ypres battle. The guns are 6 inch howitzers firing breech loading ammunition which had a separate cordite propellant charge. The copper driving rings at the base of the shell engage with the rifling in the barrel of the gun ensuring the shell is spun when it is fired
(IWM EA 4606)

There are three distinct parts to the production of munitions: the construction of the 'container' – be it shell, bomb or depth charge; the manufacture of the container to close engineering tolerances; the production of the explosive; and the filling of the container with the explosive, the most labour intensive of the three parts. During the First World War the provision of the 'container' element was effected by expanding existing engineering firms which became Controlled Establishments as well as through imports. The increase in the production of explosives required the development of new factories, the first of which was at Oldbury (West Midlands), which produced TNT, and the modification of existing explosive manufacturing plants, as at Penrhyndeudraeth (Gwynedd)[8] which produced both TNT and picric acid.[9] For the final stage, some filling factories were constructed on greenfield sites (as at Rotherwas) and others by taking over existing factory buildings.

The British chemical industry lagged well behind that of Germany in the development of high explosives. At the beginning of the war the British armed forces were still using picric acid – usually known in this country as lyddite, as their main explosive, having only approved the use of TNT in 1909. Lyddite is far from ideal as a shell filling as it reacts with metals to form dangerously unstable picrates. It is difficult to detonate, particularly when wet, leading to frequent misfires. Yet when it does explode, it produces a thick black smoke which can make it difficult to see exactly where the shell has landed. A further problem was that ammunition dumps are liable to explode *en masse* if hit by a single shell, the same defect meaning that lyddite filled shells explode on contact with armoured plate rather than penetrate it. This latter shortcoming was cruelly exposed at the Battle of Jutland in 1916 when the German fleet sank more ships than did the British despite being the inferior force in terms of ship and gun numbers. German shells were filled with TNT as from 1902 and these penetrated British armour before exploding.[10]

TNT had been tested in Britain in 1902 and again in 1905 but was rejected as insufficiently powerful. It is a difficult explosive to detonate, indeed in 1910 it was exempted from the provisions of the 1875 Explosives Act.[11] Its advantages were finally appreciated in 1913 and by the start of the war TNT had been adopted as the principal explosive resulting in the production of lyddite being run down. TNT manufacture had begun at Ardeer (Scotland) in 1907 but output was low. At the start of the war the Germans were firing off 2,500 tons of TNT each week when in the UK the total production of both TNT and lyddite was less than 20 tons per week! The shortfalls this left were filled with imports; Du Ponts in the United States were to produce almost 1,000,000 tons of TNT during the war.[12] TNT was made to go as far as possible by diluting it with ammonium nitrate to produce amatol. Grades of amatol containing up to 60% ammonium nitrate could be melted and poured into shells, a similar process to filling shells with lyddite but unlike that for pure TNT which could not be melted by hot water or steam. The 80/20 amatol adopted in April 1915 required the development of a new, cold filling, process, but subsequent experiments to develop a new hot fill process were carried out in Unit 1 of the Southern Section at Rotherwas.[13]

British First World War artillery was divided into quick firing and breech loading guns. Quick firing ammunition were one piece shells with the propellant charge held in a brass cartridge case attached to the explodable shell. The cartridge cases were reused as many as 12 times before being melted down. Guns using quick firing ammunition could keep up a rate of fire of between 15 and 20 rounds a minute. Breech loading shells were considerably bigger and were loaded into the gun with a separate propellant charge usually contained in a silk bag. Rates of fire were slower, with the bigger guns needing to load their shells using a chain lift. The dividing line between the two types of shell was at 4.5 inch, with shells of that size or above being of the breech loading type.

To fire a shell there are in fact two explosives needed: a low explosive used as a propellant, and a high explosive to burst the container. When set off both convert a solid mass (occasionally a liquid as with nitro-glycerine) into a very much larger volume of gas, the difference being the rate at which they do it. The high explosive charge in a shell must not be too sensitive for it has to withstand the stresses of being rapidly accelerated along the barrel of a gun. Neither lyddite or amatol are easy to set off and need some form of more easily exploded detonator as an intermediary explosive between the main charge and the fuze. Detonation of a shell or bomb begins with the exploding of the fuze. It in turn explodes the detonator filled with highly sensitive explosives such as mercury fulminate or lead azide. Fuzes of shells are armed at or just before the time of use, whilst bombs are armed just before loading on to an aircraft; it is dangerous to have a fuzed shell or bomb hanging around, as all that is needed to set it off is a blow on the nose. The section arming and connecting cartridge cases to filled shells would screw a primer into the base of the cartridge case which would be detonated by the firing pin striking it. Rotherwas in the First World War only filled breech loading shells with a minimum calibre of 4.5 inches. The 1930s modernisation provided facilities on the Northern Section where filled shells from the Southern Section were attached to brass cartridge cases holding a cordite charge to produce a ready-to-fire quick firing round.

Fuzes are a vital part of any munition. At the beginning of the war British fuzes were extremely unreliable, often either failing to explode at all or doing so at the wrong time. It has been suggested that during the bombardment before the Battle of the Somme in June 1916 around one third of the breech loading ammunition used failed to explode. The type 106 fuze introduced in late 1916 was the first successful British instant impact fuze.

The problem of exploding gas shells at the correct height above the ground was never successfully solved during the war, the solution employed being similar to the time fuze used with shrapnel shells. Exploded above the ground using a relatively small explosive charge, the shrapnel balls travelled forward and were very effective against troops out in the open. (Against a well entrenched enemy one officer described them as less effective than rain, which was at least wet.) However, the first gases used were asphyxiating ones, discharged from cylinders brought up to the front line, the gas being released when wind conditions would carry it to the enemy's trenches.

Gas was not a novel weapon – the use of asphyxiating gases had been controlled by the 1907 Hague Convention. Specifically this banned the use of sulphur dioxide, a gas produced when sulphur is set alight and which was used to clear a building of enemy troops. The Convention did not foresee the use of chlorine and the Allies quickly dropped their objection to its use by Germany once they too had begun to use it. Chlorine was first successfully employed by the Germans against the French on 22 April 1915. Chlorine is a vesical gas which when inhaled causes choking. The lungs react by producing liquid and the victim may die from drowning. But there were tremendous problems in using gas in cylinders, apart from relying on the right weather conditions. The logistics of supplying anything to the front line trenches was a nightmare, with everything having to be manhandled for the last mile or so. The detection of any movement behind the enemy's trenches was the signal to start an artillery bombardment and this generally limited supply to night time. Each gas cylinder containing chlorine weighed around 125lb and required four people to carry it.

Later gas shells were filled with liquid poisonous gasses which were effective when absorbed through the skin. These shells were provided with a small explosive burster charge with the intention of exploding them a few feet above the ground and spreading the liquid over a wide area. But shells containing asphyxiant or lachrymatory (tear gas) agents failed to deliver gas in sufficient concentrations to be effective – a barrage no matter how heavy could not match the tonnage of these gases delivered from cylinders. To try to overcome this, the British developed the Livens Projector, a crude and inaccurate trench mortar which fired a simple cylinder containing around 10 litres (2 gallons) of gas and a small burster charge. The projectors were dug in well behind the front line trenches and several hundred would be fired

A Livens Projector being loaded with gas canisters each of which held 10 litres of poison gas, usually phosgene, with a small burster charge. The weapon's inaccuracy did not matter as it was used to saturate an area with gas with as many as a thousand projectors dug in well behind the British trenches and all fired together (IWM Q14945)

at the same moment. Perhaps the most successful such attack was when 2,300 Livens Projectors were used against the Germans on 4 April 1917.

Undoubtedly the most 'successful' gas developed during the war was mustard gas. The Germans first used their version, Yperite, in July 1917. It is almost odourless, producing delayed-action symptoms of severe internal and external blistering causing vomiting and often death as it can also be absorbed through the skin. The introduction of mustard gas brought about a fundamental change in trench warfare. Together with improvements in correctly registering guns on their targets without firing ranging shots, here at last was a method whereby the enemy's guns could be silenced before an attack. Mustard gas persists in the soil or on the surface of an object for several weeks. This persistence, together with its strength and its ability to soak into objects, meant that small quantities added to high explosive shells were effective. In a period of six weeks from 12 July 1917 German gas attacks against the British trenches were nearly continuous. At a time when casualties were measured in miles of graves the resulting 694 deaths were neither here nor there, but 16,000 men were incapacitated, many of them permanently blinded.[14] Edward Spiers, in *Chemical Warfare*, describes mustard gas as 'a weapon of area denial'[15] and by 1918 all the belligerents were convinced of its effectiveness, to the extent that they were planning that in 1919 between one third and one half of all ammunition would be shells charged with mustard gas. More than half of all the gas produced in the UK during the war was manufactured in 1918 – 65,160 tons out of a total of 124,200 tons.[16]

Prior to 1914 this country had imported most of the chemicals needed by industry from Germany and thus had to develop a chemical industry of its own. Lack of skills in this field produced a considerable delay in the introduction of mustard gas after it was identified following its use by the Germans in April 1917. In fact the problems of producing mustard gas were not completely solved until 1940.[17] The first UK attempts to produce it were at Chittening but the gas produced contained free sulphur which resulted in blocked pipework. Due to massive contamination the factory was closed in April 1918 and work began on a greenfield site at Avonmouth. By the time this closed on Armistice Day it had produced just 560 tons of gas[18] at the cost of a large number of casualties to the extent that at times 70% of the workforce was incapacitated. (A factory casualty, in the parlance of the time, was someone who was off work for more than three days.)[19] The only successful commercial firm to produce mustard gas was Levenstein in Manchester.[20] Unit 2 at Banbury (Oxfordshire) Filling Factory was altered to allow mustard gas charging in July 1918 and in October, just five weeks before the war ended, Unit 1 of the lyddite section at Rotherwas began to charge shells.[21]

The huge and rapid development of the munitions industry during the war generated consequential changes in society. The sheer scale of the operation was larger than almost any other United Kingdom industrial operation, with a workforce bigger than most other UK employers. By the end of the First World War the Ministry of Munitions was supervising the operations of some 20,000 manufacturing establishments.

The government's Health of Munitions Committee, appointed in the autumn of 1915, produced a series of reports which was to profoundly influence the whole of industry and the National Factories. (These latter were owned and run by the government, unlike Controlled Establishments which remained in private ownership.) The National Factories became leaders in the provision of welfare facilities. Among other things the committee looked at industrial fatigue, industrial diseases, food and dietary matters, juvenile employment and safe working practices. One conclusion led to the provision of specific welfare conditions both in and outside the factory including the introduction of accident books, detailed suggestions as to what washing and sanitary facilities should be provided, guidelines as to the hours each class of workers should work and banning the employment of juveniles on night shifts. Perhaps its most important work was to recognise the dangers of TNT poisoning and to lay down guidelines to counter it. Female welfare supervisors were appointed at all National Factories.[22] The Committee also suggested a shorter working week which resulted in higher productivity figures and also improved quality.[23] Indeed, many of the social benefits and controls over working conditions enjoyed by today's workers stem from this committee's recommendations.

Employment in the combined Controlled Establishments and National Factories grew from 77,000 in July 1914 to 329,000 in July 1918 with the number of females employed rising from 2,000 to 276,000.[24] As the war continued, the demands of the armed forces for men to replace those killed or injured could only be met by taking men away from industry, in turn replaced by women and to a lesser extent by juveniles.[25] This introduction of large numbers of women into relatively well paid employment marked a major step in their eventual emancipation. In return for Emmeline and Sylvia Pankhurst's agreement to suspend suffragette activities and their cooperation in the Right to Serve March of 17 July 1915, Lloyd George promised the vote to the Women's Social and Political Union. Parliament eventually endorsed this in January 1918.[26] Many of the females employed in the munitions industry on the whole came from other industries, those new to factory work often taking jobs in commercial industries, or clerical posts.[27]

The development at Rotherwas in 1916 brought with it a novel situation which provided the area with both opportunities and problems. For the first time the young women of the area were offered an alternative to domestic service or marriage with the prospect of earning high wages, whilst the influx of female industrial workers from elsewhere who took employment at Rotherwas had a considerable impact on the city of Hereford, and not just because of the novelty of the development.

According to the 1911 census Hereford had a population of 22,568 whilst the 1921 census lists just 5,566 houses, highlighting the problems of finding lodgings for the large immigrant labour force that came to work at Rotherwas. When the site was being considered the possibility of a shortage of labour was raised but the manager of the local employment exchange replied that providing recruitment extended into South Wales there would be no problem, a prophesy proved wrong in both wars. The Mayor of Hereford stated in the autumn of 1916 that the city was to be invaded by 'women the like of which the city had never seen before'.[28]

2   The Early History of the Site[1]

The Domesday Book records Rotherwas as being held by Sigeric before 1066, after the Norman Conquest it became the property of Gilbert, son of Thorold, who owned other manors in Herefordshire. Rotherwas was a part of the parish and the hundred of Dinedor and at the time of the survey was called *Retrowas*. It had a population of 10 villagers and boasted 13 ploughs. Valued at £6 before the Conquest, in the Domesday survey in 1089 its value had halved to £3. The village is not mentioned by Blount who, writing in 1675, only described Rotherwas House and its park.[2] A number of medieval villages in Herefordshire vanished as a consequence of the Black Death and Rotherwas may be among them – the county's Sites and Monuments Record notes earthworks (SO 533 365) to the west of the site of Rotherwas House (SO 536 384) which could be the site of the village of *Retrowas*. It is possible that the fish pond (SO 534 382) south-west of Rotherwas House originally supplied Friday's dinner for the village.[3]

Rotherwas was acquired by the Bodenham family in 1483, becoming their principal seat. The construction of the chapel is credited to Sir Roger Bodenham (1545-1623) who had converted to Catholicism after being 'cured' of leprosy following a visit to St. Winifred's Well in Flintshire. A Victorian stained-glass window in the chapel dedicated to the saint, records this event. Sir Roger also added a stone wing to the house.

During the Civil War the family supported the King and the property was seized in 1646 by the Parliamentarians. It was used by them for a few years and then seemingly abandoned. Many of the buildings became derelict and were to remain so for several decades. The family fortunes improved after the Restoration, and in 1732 Sir Charles Bodenham was able to build an 11-bay brick mansion designed by James Gibbs, next to the stone wing which he converted into estate offices. The last of the family, another Charles Bodenham, inherited the estate in 1865 and made improvements to both house and chapel, the latter in 1868 costing £750 and believed to have been overseen by Edward Pugin. Charles de la Barre Bodenham married the Countess Irena Maria, daughter of a Polish count and she inherited the estate when her husband died in 1883. In 1884 she rebuilt the east end of the chapel in memory of her husband. Having no direct heirs, on her death in 1892 the property passed to her cousin, Count Lubienski, who changed his name to Lubienski-Bodenham. The estate ran into severe financial problems and after Count Lubienski's death on 19 March 1909[4] it was put up for sale, although there is the record of an unsuccessful attempt to run Rotherwas House as a hydro during 1912. It failed to sell in one lot and an auction was held at the Green Dragon Hotel on 5 September 1912 when Edwards, Russell & Baldwin sold the 2,578 acres, dividing the sale into 76 lots.[5] Lot 68 included Rotherwas House, two cottages and a range of farm buildings, 4 miles of salmon fishing rights along the Wye, the pleasure gardens with a separate walled garden running down to the river and 195 acres. Twenty-five of the lots, including lot 68, failed to reach their reserve and were advertised for sale in the

Rotherwas Chapel (Ron Shoesmith)

Hereford Times during October 1912. Lot 68 was offered at £15,000. In the end the lot was split, with 185 acres being bought by Hereford County Council to be used as allotments and smallholdings, with Rotherwas House and its immediate surroundings being sold to a Mr. Mayhew who is perhaps best described as an asset stripper.

Soon after the house was sold the *Hereford Times* reported that the agent for the Bodenham Estate had obtained Home Office permission to remove the remains of those buried in and around the chapel and described what was being done as 'little more than licensed sacrilege'. Two men were engaged in pulling down the altar, the intention of the new owner – 'a gentleman well known to business circles in Hereford' – being to demolish the chapel. This building, they wrote, resembled a charnel house – 'an apartment of bones with the remains of 39 people of whom some 19 have been identified'. Those disinterred ran from Maria Bodenham who died on 7 June 1691, to Irena de la Bodenham who died on 10 December 1892, as well as Thomas Hildeyard, an 18th-century clockmaker who had built the chapel's clock. This clock, known as Old Father Hildeyard, has since disappeared. This was the second disinterment for Charles de la Barre Bodenham. On his death in 1882 he had been buried in the graveyard outside, there being no space in the chapel. His widow had a small side chapel added to the main building and then had her husband's body removed by two estate workers to a vault where later she was also buried.[6] She built St. Charles House, designed by Pugin and Pugin at Lower Bullingham. This was a charity refuge home with six sets of rooms each large enough for a family.[7] This time Charles de le Barre Bodenham's bones, together with those of his relations, were re-interred in a small burial ground (SO 537 380) on land which had been retained by the Lubienski family.[8] This wasn't the last indignity to be heaped on the chapel – in 1926 it was being used a potato store.

On 11 March 1913 there began a four day auction sale of the contents of Rotherwas House which was conducted by the London auctioneers, Osborn & Mercher, a sale sufficiently important to be advertised in a special supplement to *Country Life*.[9] The auction included furniture by Adam, Chippendale and Sheraton, early English mirrors and clocks, a specimen bordered tapestry panel (of a hunting screen) and rare old panellings and carvings, together with the mantelpieces, overmantels and doors to the principal rooms in walnut, oak and other woods. The panelling and wooden carvings were sold to Amherst College, Massachusetts, an organisation founded by an American oil magnate, C.M. Pratt. Amherst College's website mentions the Rotherwas room at the college and remarks on its magnificent walnut panelling. The sale notice stated that the firm had also been instructed to sell by auction on 14 March 1914 the house itself, the gardens and some land, in all about ten acres, mentioning that the house was ideal for conversion to an institution, college or residential hotel and included 1.5 miles of fishing rights on the Wye. No record of this sale has been found, but when the land for the filling factory was bought by the Ministry of Munitions in 1916, Rotherwas House and ten acres of land was purchased from a Mr. E.A. Taylor.[10]

Meanwhile, in early January 1913, the *Hereford Times* was able to report on an acrimonious debate in the city council concerning their purchase of the land around Rotherwas House at a cost of £8,000. Speakers suggested that the supposed demand for 100 smallholdings which had prompted the purchase was a false figure, and that only 10 at most were firm applications.[11]

The Filling Factory

In 1915, the first phase of the expansion in national munitions production had concentrated on engineering facilities and explosive manufacture, with the provision of filling factories coming later. By April 1916, however, the Ministry of Munitions had built three filling factories to produce large, breech-loading shells.[12] These were at Banbury (Oxfordshire), where shells were filled with lyddite, and Morecambe (Lancashire) and Chillwell (Nottingham) where amatol was used as the explosive charge.[13] On 25 April 1916 Eric Geddes,[14] the industrialist Lloyd George had brought in to the Ministry of Munitions as his deputy, and who later became a member of his cabinet, gave instructions for a suitable site to be found for a fourth factory. This factory was initially intended as an insurance against anything going awry with the existing factories. The proof that this was a wise decision came in October 1917 when a fire destroyed much of the factory at Morecambe. It reopened as a wood distillation plant and later charged gas and smoke shells. Further proof came on 1 July 1918 when an explosion at Chillwell reduced output there,[15] and killed 134 people.[16]

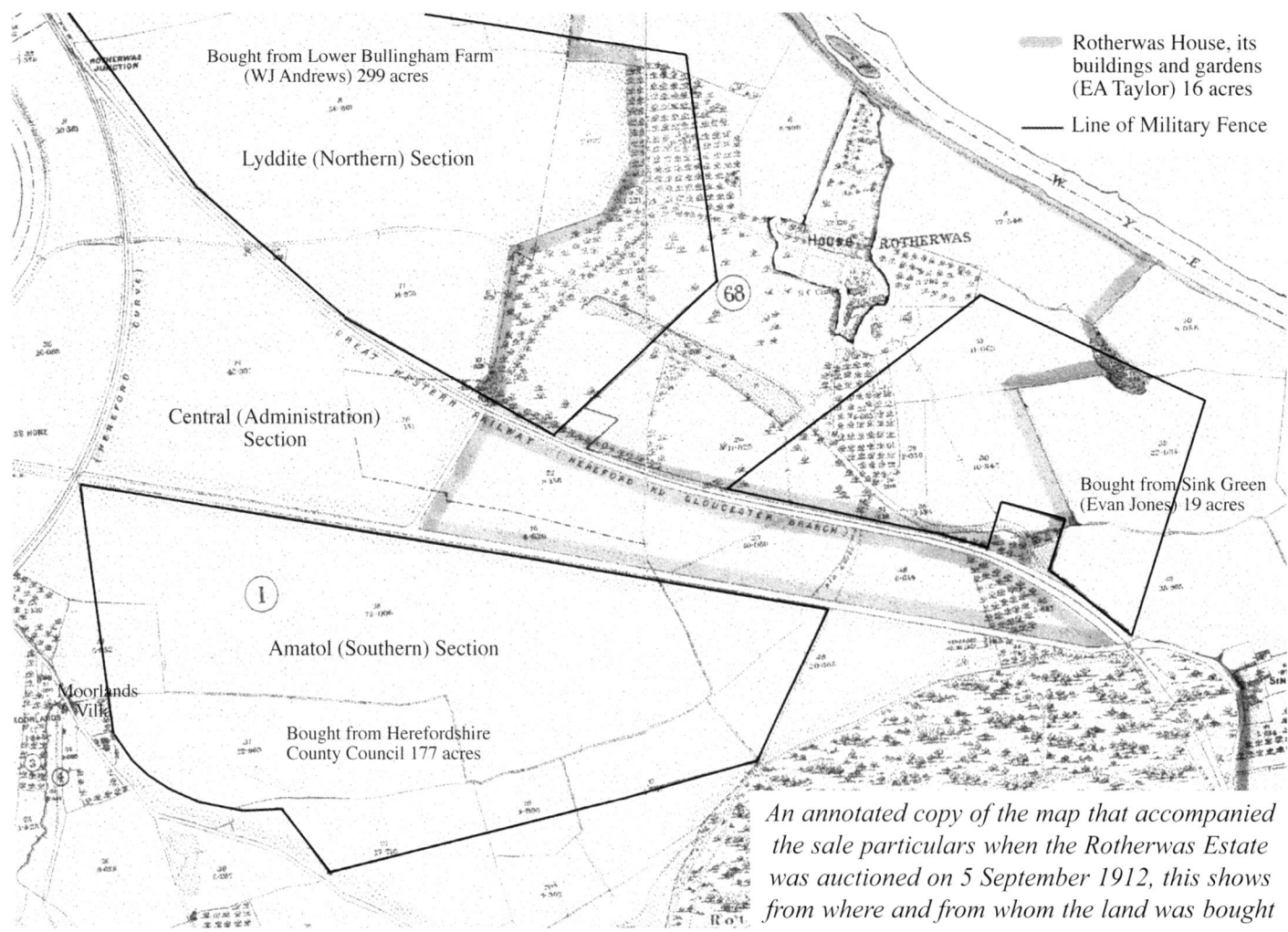

An annotated copy of the map that accompanied the sale particulars when the Rotherwas Estate was auctioned on 5 September 1912, this shows from where and from whom the land was bought

As early as January 1916, the *Hereford Times* had reported that a munitions factory might be coming to Hereford. The city council, worried that people were leaving the town to go and work in Birmingham, had canvassed the Ministry of Munitions trying to get them to establish a government controlled factory in the town. The report in the *Hereford Times* considered that the county was the only one without a munitions factory, and suggested that an existing factory would be taken over.[17]

Late in May 1916 a site of some 545 acres at Rotherwas was chosen.[18] The site offered several advantages: it was level – the actual fall across the site from west to east is only 1 foot 1 inch,[19] whilst the river Wye forming the northern boundary was both a natural barrier and the supplier of the large volumes of process water needed. Yet the land was said to be flood free. There was an existing railway network, with the GWR line from Hereford to Ross on Wye, running through the site from the north-west corner to the centre of the eastern boundary. This joined the joint LNWR / GWR line at Rotherwas Junction (SO 523 388) where the former curved away westwards towards Abergavenny. There was also a road link, for running through the centre of the site from east to west was the Hereford to Holme Lacy road, which subsequently became the B4849. Mains water, gas and electricity were all available.[20] However, the deciding factor was undoubtedly that the site was underlain with what the official history describes as 'an inexhaustible supply of gravel and sand'. The amount of gravel required was so huge that had they had to bring it in from elsewhere, construction of the factory would have been severely delayed. There was also a desperate shortage of railway trucks at the time – construction began just days after the Somme offensive was launched. As it was, more than 20,000 truck loads of materials were delivered to Rotherwas during its construction.[21]

The original intention was that the factory would have a capacity to handle 400 tons of amatol and 200 tons of lyddite each week, but before the drawings went out to tender this was increased to 700 tons of amatol and 400 tons of lyddite, necessitating changes to the factory layout.[22] As built, the Northern, lyddite, Section consisted of two factories (Units 1 and 2), each the mirror image of the other's layout. The amatol units on the Southern Section, as originally planned, were designed to handle 60/40 amatol – 60% ammonium nitrate and 40% TNT. However, during the time the factory was being built, a new cold filling process was developed at Woolwich to use 80/20 amatol and introduced at the Chillwell National Filling Factory.[23] 60/40 amatol was produced by heating the ammonium nitrate to above the melting point of TNT and then mixing the two chemicals; 80/20 was produced by milling the two chemicals together and gave an explosive with a higher explosive velocity that was easier to set off. It was this that Hereford was now needed to produce, and it meant that Units 2 to 7 of the Southern Section had to be completely redesigned. Unit 1 was too near to completion to be altered and it was turned into an experimental hot-fill line for the new amatol. The other six units, divided in three pairs, each with their associated ammonium nitrate store, were constructed to use the cold-fill process. Additionally, it was decided to erect six Army Ordnance Depot (AOD) stores at Rotherwas, each 178 x 120ft, and a further ten stores, each 180

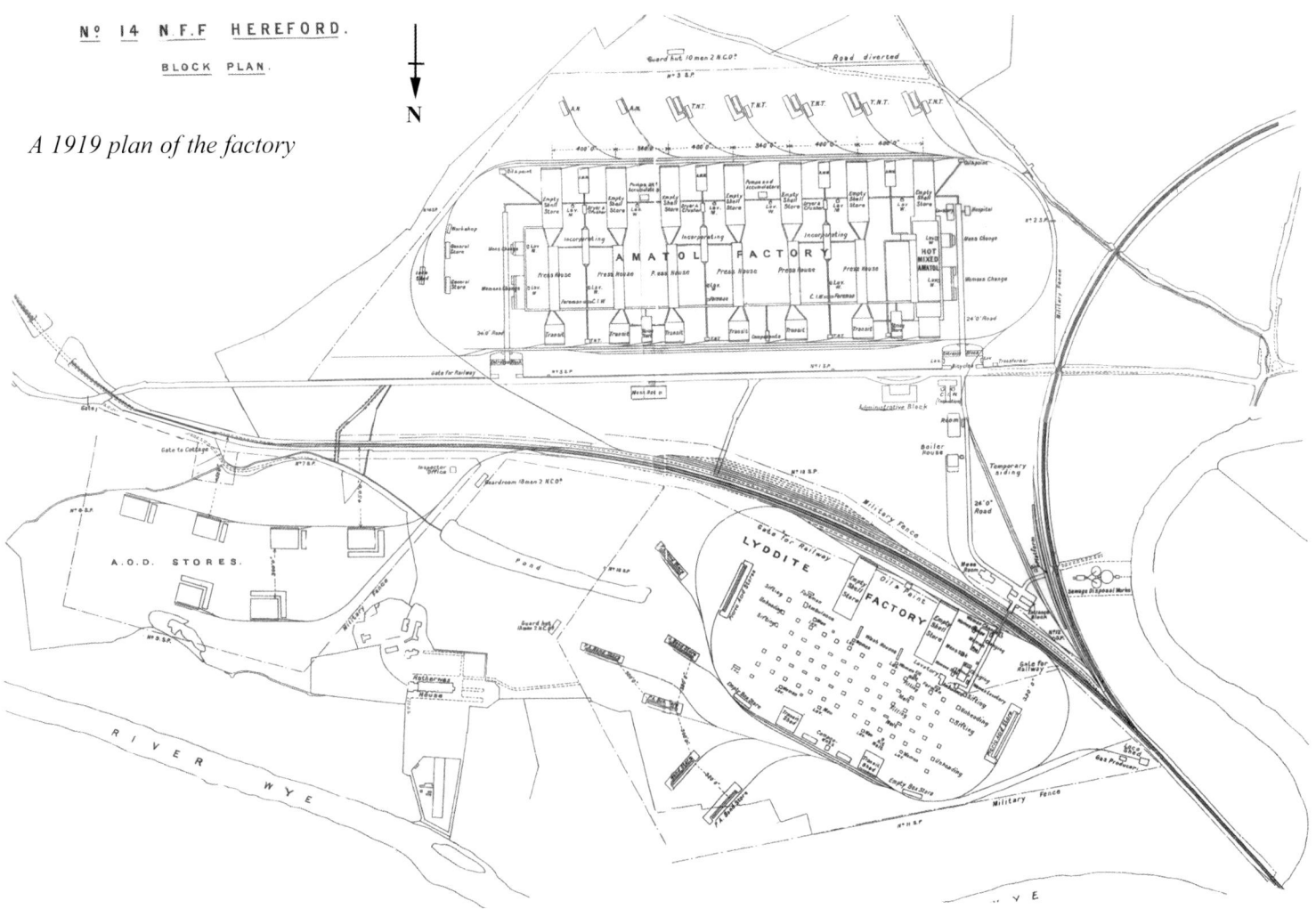

A 1919 plan of the factory

A photograph taken during the construction of the lyddite section, circa *1916. All the buildings were connected by a series of wooden floored corridors, roofed over and partly walled in. The row of buildings to the left of the corridor are fill houses, each with a lean-to to allow delivery and dispatch of shells in the dry. Further to the left, with long roof ventillators, are the melt houses. To the right is a kit house holding supplies of bees wax, used to seal the explosive in a shell. The corridor floors supported a Decauville narrow gauge railway and a turntable was situated just to the right of the figure in the foreground. Amazingly this complex set of buildings became operational just four months after building work began (PRO MUN 5/306)*

x 120ft, together with offices, on a 150 acre site at Credenhill (SO 45 44), a village six miles west-north-west of Hereford and served from the Hereford to Hay-on-Wye, LNWR line. As with Rotherwas, aggregate was available on the chosen site. Each filling factory was provided with storage to hold six weeks production.[24] The scheme also provided for alterations to Rotherwas House, to turn it into an army barracks for those guarding the site, and for the construction of hostel accommodation at Hereford for those building the factory. No evidence, however, has been found that any such hostel accommodation was built. Barracks were provided at Credenhill and some First World War buildings survive there.[25]

The land was acquired on 15 June 1916 but the Office of Works had already commenced work on preparing the required 3,000 drawings that included numerous details.[26] The documentation regarding the amatol section went out to tender on 12 June and for the lyddite section three days later. While the documents and plans were out to tender, staff from the Office of Works were on site setting out the buildings. At the same time the gravel pits were opened up.[27]

The construction contract was awarded to James Mowlem & Co. Ltd. at £1,200,000, and was signed on 5 July when work had already begun on construction of the rail link by GWR workers. A photograph in the Public Record Office dated 24 May 1916 shows the construction gang building rail lines. A resident architect, Mr. J.F. Milne, was employed.[28]

It seems that the original plan was to complete the building of one unit of both the Southern, amatol, and of the Northern, lyddite, Sections as quickly as possible and to begin filling shells. This would allow workers to be trained up and to enable skilled staff to be transferred to the next units as they came on line.

Unit 1 of the lyddite factory filled its first shell on 11 November, exactly two years to the day before the armistice was signed.[29] The redesign of the amatol section delayed completion of these units, resulting in the first shell containing 80/20 amatol being pressed on 22 June 1917 in Unit 2 and during the first week 875, 8 inch shells were filled. Completion of all but Unit 1 was achieved in about 14 months from the date work began on site.[30] Limited production in Unit 1 using the experimental hot fill process for 80/20 amatol began in March 1918 but full production was not reached until November 1918.[31]

The amatol factory and the AOD stores consisted in the main of steel-framed structures with inner hollow tile filling, corrugated iron roofs, and with the outer walls being covered with roughcast concrete. The buildings were to be fireproof as far as possible; to provide the highest degree of safety and hygienic conditions that skill could devise.[32] So far as can be ascertained, the TNT magazines on the Southern Section were constructed in a similar manner, except that the walling here was 13.5 inch brickwork. Materials used in constructing the factory included 5,000 tons of steelwork, 12.25 million bricks, 16,300 tons of cement, 1,500,000 feet 'super' of hollow walling blocks, 1,500 tons of corrugated iron, 3,250 'standards' of timber, and 600,000 tons of sand and gravel dug on site.[33] The site was provided with 27 miles of standard gauge railway track, 3 miles of roads, 9 miles of military fencing with 16 sentry posts along it, 10 miles of footpaths and

Left: The Bustin photograph taken from Dinedor Hill showing the Southern, amatol, Section, thought to be circa *1917, with the TNT magazines incomplete and with no earth traverses yet constructed. The stacks of the boiler house can be seen in the centre background and provide some idea of what a huge area is covered by the site. Centre: This enlargement shows an ammonium nitrate store with an empty shell store to the left. Right: An enlargement of the incomplete TNT magazine for Unit 6*

sentry paths and some 370 buildings, including three guard houses manned on a permanent basis. The largest buildings on the site were the nine empty shell stores. A survey of the surviving empty shell store of the Northern Section (SO 527 376) produced dimensions of 356.5 x 120ft, just 87 square yards short of an acre.[34]

A wet plate negative from the Bustin collection, held at Hereford Record Office, taken from an elevated position on Dinedor hill looks over the Southern Section.[35] It is undated but is thought to have been taken late in the construction period, c.1917. It contains evidence for a narrow gauge railway – a carpenter working on the site was killed when knocked down by a narrow gauge railway engine – but raises doubts as to which of the TNT magazines were provided with protective earthen embankments or traverses. Magazines 2 to 5 inclusive were undoubtedly completed by November 1918, but later map evidence shows, in one case, stores 1 and 7 without an earth traverse and in another, 6 and 7 are named as ammonium nitrate stores. This seems unlikely as ammonium nitrate is deliquescent – taking up moisture from the atmosphere and turning into a liquid – and specialist stores were built. The earth traverses ringing each magazine on the three most vulnerable sides were designed to direct a possible explosion upwards, but there was a rail access cut through one side. These rail cuttings are just wide enough to allow entry of the rail trucks and are vertically sided with cast-in-situ concrete. The traverses at Banbury had similar cuttings but these were lined with brick on the open side and on that which abutted the earth traverse, and then centrally filled with concrete.[36]

The design of the empty shell stores and transit sheds on both sections were similar, but many of the buildings on the Northern Section, where lyddite was handled, were wooden-framed buildings, covered in weatherboard and roofed with corrugated iron. The original plans were for the roof to be wooden covered with tarred felt, by no means a fireproof covering, as the fire in 1917 which destroyed the Morecambe Filling Factory proved.[37]

The 1919 map on page 14 suggests that only canteens, the boiler house, a hospital and the administration centre (SO 525 381) were put up in the Central Section which lay between the lyddite and amatol sections, before the end of the war.[38] A map dated 1924 suggests that a number of other buildings in the Central Section which pre-date the Second World War modernization, were built some time between the end of the war and 1932, possibly in more than one tranche.[39]

Drainage was difficult because the site is so level. A sewage works was established on the western edge (strangely at almost the furthest possible point upstream) and in total some 22 miles of drains were installed.[40] A fire fighting mains, which led through

This Bustin photograph, never previously published, is taken from the north side of the River Wye. It looks towards the Northern, lyddite, Section. Rail trucks are stood outside the picric acid expense store to the right and the wooden floored, covered corridors connecting the buildings are clearly visible. In the background, to the right, are the twin stacks of the boiler house

the whole of the factory complex, was fed in the first instance from a reservoir on Dinedor Hill (SO 531 521) to the south-east of the site. The site was also connected to the town waterworks.[41] Additionally, a pumping plant capable of supplying up to 600 gallons/minute was constructed on the banks of the river.[42] Map evidence shows that water from the Hereford water works at Broomy Hill was brought in to the site via a 4 inch main.

Electric power, used both as a motive source and for lighting, was drawn from the Hereford Corporation plant which then had a capacity of 4,000 KW. It was delivered to the site at 3,000 volts and transformed down to 400 volt, three phase, or 230 volt, single phase. The power required by the factory led the Ministry of Munitions to spend £100,000 on extending the corporation's electricity works. In 1919 the council exercised their option to buy the extension and were able to begin to extend the area in and around the city which was supplied with electricity.[43]

The filling of shells in the Northern Section required that the lyddite be melted using oil baths heated by gas generated in a gas producer plant sited in the far north-western corner of the site (SO 524 386). Producer gas, a mixture of hydro-carbon gases, is obtained by passing a controlled mixture of steam and air through a furnace burning any one of a number of carbon based fuels, such as coal, wood or charcoal. It was process developed in the middle of the 19th century and by the beginning of the 20th a producer gas plant and an associated internal combustion engine were commonly used to provide power at remote sites such as quarries.[44] Presumably for safety reasons this building was in a very isolated position, resulting in a supply main of at least 500 yards to the nearest melt houses of the lyddite unit. Quite how reliable this supply was is open to question as the oil baths used to melt the lyddite are described as having pilot lights using gas taken from Hereford's town gas supply, with the heat for melting being produced from the producer gas plant. The whole of the factory complex was heated from a boiler house (SO 527 384), installed in the Central Section. It employed eight, coal-fired, Lancashire boilers and fed steam into a main supply pipeline of $1^1/_2$ miles in length.[45] It was housed in a building with a Belfast truss roof and had twin chimney stacks.[46]

The Construction Workers
The labour force used in building the factory was drawn from the army itself (around 250 men), together with some 500 navvies and 1,500 superior workmen, artisans and mechanics.[47] Accommodation for them was a problem. When the factory was first mooted, the mayor had dismissed doubts that the city could find lodgings for these immigrant workers, saying that the city had found digs for a large number of newly enlisted soldiers in the early part of the war and could do so again. In June 1916 the mayor wrote to the *Hereford Times* announcing that there was to be an immediate influx of a large number of workers and that they would need lodgings. He urged any city residents who could help to get in touch with the manager of the local labour exchange.

Despite a similar letter from the factory manager, Mr. Greenland, the response to these appeals was insufficient to meet the needs for accommodation and suitable premises were commandeered and fitted out for occupation as workmen's hostels. One of these buildings was the garage premises of the Hereford Motor Co. in Eign Street, Hereford – now Steels of Hereford. The company advertised in the *Hereford Times*, stating that, as the Ministry of Munitions had taken over their St. George's Garage, they had moved to 33 Broad Street.[48] Later they asked the Defence of the Realm, Losses Commission, for £550 to cover the use of their St. George's Garage between 31 July 1916 and 1 February 1917, but they were awarded just £180.[49] The Church Army set up and ran an on-site canteen for the construction workers using £400 it had in its Hut Fund, but they were refused permission to staff the factory canteen.[50] By mid-1916 the construction and running of canteens for government establishments had been officially taken over by the Ministry of Munitions.[51]

As soon as the construction of Unit 1 on the amatol section was completed, the buildings began to be used as hostel accommodation and recreation facilities for those building the factory – rather than acting as a training centre for workers as had been planned. A cinema and a skittle alley were added, the costs being all but covered from the profits of a bar selling beer established on the site.[52]

There is evidence that many of the construction workers came from Ireland. The *Hereford Times* and the *Hereford Journal* between July 1916 and through to the end of 1917, contain regular reports of Irishmen brought before the magistrates court for being drunk and disorderly.[53]

An amendment to the Defence of the Realm Act of August 1914, passed in 1915, allowed the imposition of local control of licensing hours and banned treating – the buying of a drink for anyone else. Before this there was no control of how many hours a day public houses could open. Convictions for drunkenness dropped over the period of the war. Control of licensing hours in Hereford itself, limiting opening to between 10.30 a.m. and 2.30 p.m., and 6 and 9 p.m., was brought in on Monday 25 September 1916.[54] The nearest hostelry to Rotherwas was the Wye Hotel and during the time the factory was being built this establishment was allowed to open for just one hour, at noon each day. The son of the then licensee stated that they had several galvanised baths behind the bar which were filled with beer before 12 a.m. 'The navvies,' he said, 'Came through the door four deep and four abreast'.[55]

The first labour return made by what was now designated National Filling Factory No. 14, Hereford, was on 20 November 1916, when 142 women and 57 men had been engaged to fill the first shells with lyddite.[56]

3   The Filling Operation during the First World War

There is an inherent danger in the filling of munitions where a material which is designed to explode has to be handled. In consequence the actual filling process is carried out under very strictly controlled conditions, in buildings within a secure area where entry is limited only to those whose presence is essential. At Rotherwas there were two such secure areas – a Northern Section where munitions were filled with lyddite and a larger Southern Section designed to handle amatol. Those entering the filling areas had to surrender any contraband, a term that included all forms of tobacco products including snuff, any means of lighting cigarettes, all metal objects and confectionery – the sugar in chocolate can react violently with explosives. Workers were liable to be searched to ensure they complied with the requirements. Next they would enter a separate-sex, shifting room where they would exchange their ordinary clothes for factory-provided ones which were without such items as metal buttons. They would then step over a dirty/clean barrier where they would leave their shoes and don factory provided ones. All through the secure areas there was this emphasis in separating 'dirty' and 'clean' materials in specific areas with a physical barrier erected to ensure this separation.

The actual filling process for the two explosives was very different but the process to make the shells ready for filling, and for handling then thereafter were very similar. Each unit, two on the Northern Section and seven in the Southern Section, was provided with an empty shell store and a transit shed for the filled shells, separated by the buildings where the shells were filled. The nine empty shell stores were by far the biggest buildings on the site – 356.5ft long by 120ft wide making them just a little larger than an acre. They consisted of a 14-bay north lit shed with the southernmost bay 31ft 6ins (which also contained the standard gauge railway link to the rest of the site) with all the other bays at 25ft in length. Unusually the roof was supported at the apex, not the gable, on twin channel uprights with no internal uprights at all. A gantry system using RSJs, entitled a runway on the maker's name plate, was hung from the roof. The windowless walls were infilled with 12 inch square hollow clay tiles which were spray painted with a rough concrete covering on the outside. Originally nearly all the buildings were roofed over with tar-painted corrugated iron, but this was replaced in the inter-war years with corrugated asbestos.

Empty shells were delivered to any of the shell stores by rail and were unloaded using the overhead gantry system and stored in the first one third of the building. At this end 16 runs of the gantry were set 7ft 6ins apart with a 'points' junction bringing two runs together in the central one third of the shed. Under each of the eight runways in this central section there was a work bench. On its run along the central gallery, the shells were first cleaned – rust would be wire-brushed off and grease cleaned away – before the shells would be passed over (or under for the really big shells) a barrier separating the dirty and clean parts of the bench. The shells were then painted. For lyddite filled shells painting the inside with a shellac varnish was particularly important as picric acid will react with metals to form dangerously unstable picrates.

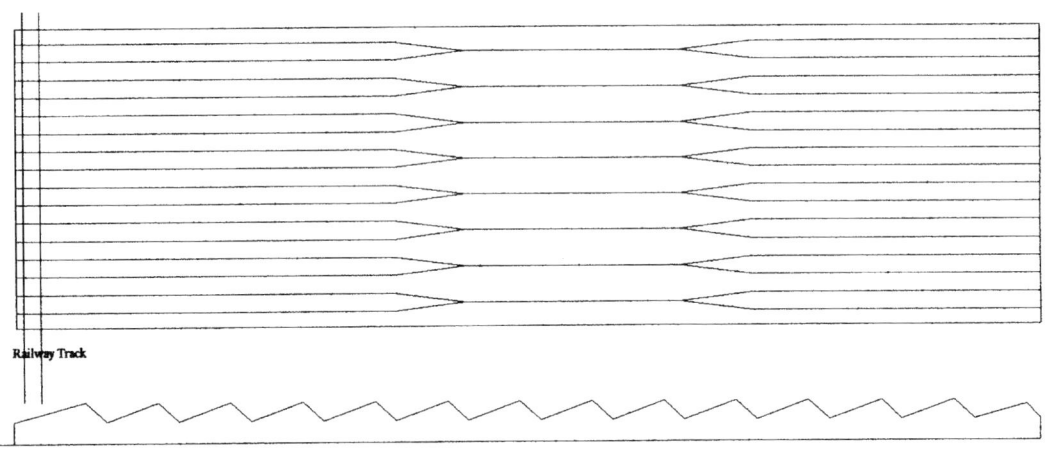

*A plan view of the gantry layout, and the rail link at the southern end of the building. In the First World War dirty shell cases would have been unloaded and stored in the southern third of the building before being delivered to working tables in the centre where they would have been cleaned and painted with the interior varnished. Once the paint had dried they would have been stood down in the northern sections of the store to await filling
(Author's survey)*

Taken in 2003 from the south-east corner this picture shows the only empty shell store to survive on the Northern Section. The gantry system is First World War vintage and the twin tracks are shown joining into one in the central part of the building. Wall ventilators are provided on both east and west walls; those on the east were provided with shutters to close them, those on the west could not be closed. These empty shell stores were a feat of engineering in themselves, covering almost an acre with no central supports, the roof carrying the gantry system

Parts of the bench were provided with heating to accelerate drying. At the end of the benches the runways again divided into two and the last third of the shed was used to store shells ready for filling. Breech loading shells were usually stored nose up with their base on the floor to prevent possible damage to the external copper drive rings which are slightly larger in diameter than the rifling in the gun barrel. As the shell is fired the drive rings engage with the grooves of the rifling forming an effective seal with the barrel to ensure the force of the propellant charge does not escape along the sides of the shells. The rifling also imparts a spin to the shell which provides a gyroscopic force to prevent it from tumbling in flight.

A view of one of the seven empty shell stores on the amatol section. In the foreground are 9.2 inch shells. They would be moved using the overhead gantry system hung from the roof, which used a points junction to bring the rails together to a single rail above the working area
(PRO MUN 5/186/1340/31)

Four internal divisions, each housing a vertical extruder, in one of the filling buildings. Shells were moved around the section on bronze-wheeled trolleys – in this case seemingly stood upright – travelling on a narrow gauge railway
(PRO MUN 5/186/1340/31)

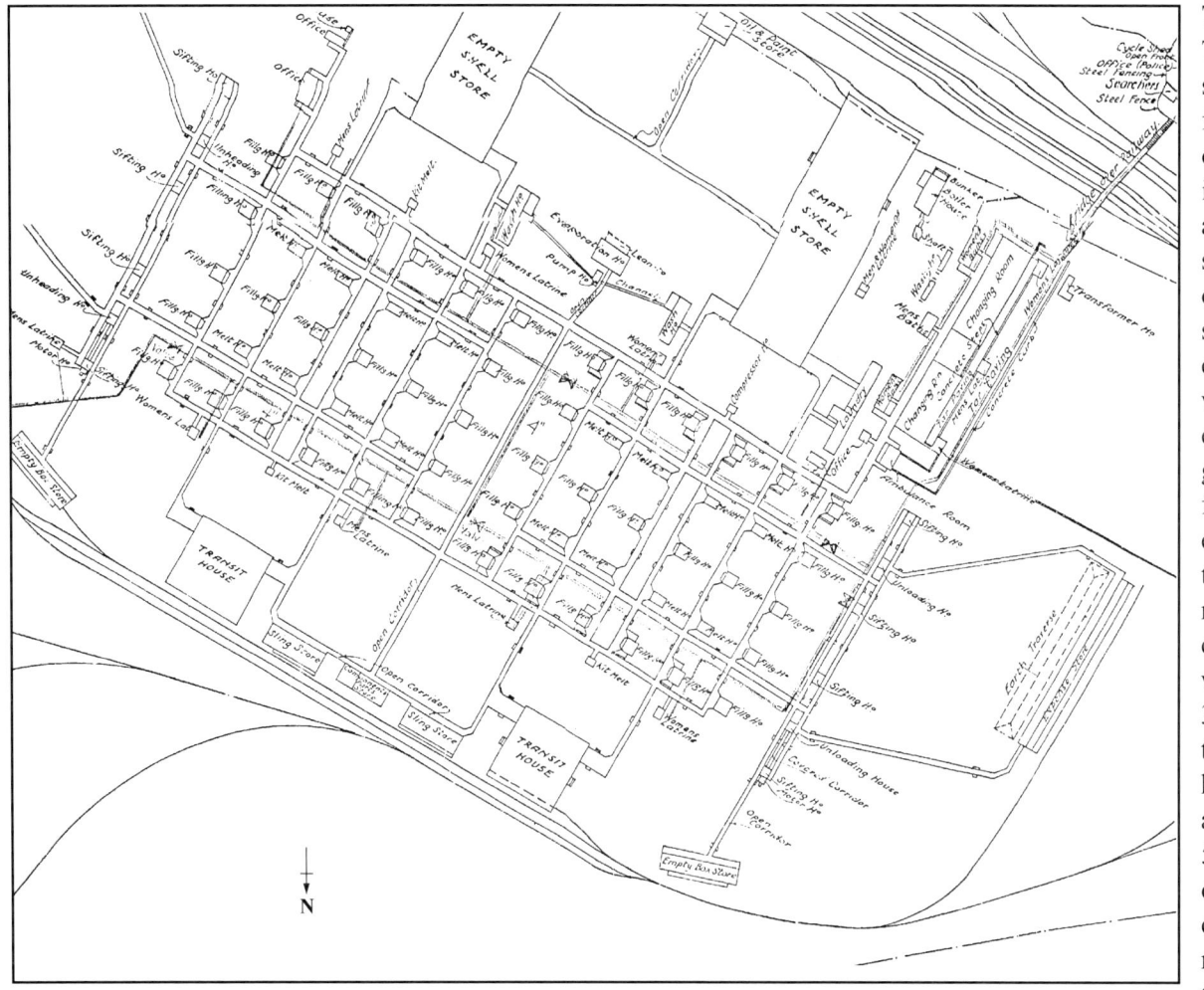

Plan of the Northern, lyddite, Section, c.1924

The Lyddite Section[1]

The lyddite section, where shells were filled with liquefied picric acid, was made up of two units each the mirror image of the other (see plan alongside). The units were supplied with picric acid from one of six bond stores (three survive) each divided into 24 cubicles separated by brick walls but with light wooden end walls and a light corrugated iron roof, so that the force from any accidental explosion would tend to be thrown upwards and outwards rather than towards the adjacent cubicles. Each cubicle was allowed to hold up to 3,000lb of explosive meaning that the whole store could hold up to 32 tons. Picric acid arrived either in 56lb boxes – 50lb if imported from Canada or the States – or in kegs containing 1cwt. When required, picric acid was taken from the bond store to one of two expense stores (one survives) each with 36 cubicles and each serving one unit of the section. With the exception of the six bond stores all the buildings on each unit was linked to all the other buildings by a series of raised, level wooden corridors. These were partly walled in corrugated iron to about 4ft high and roofed over with curved corrugated iron sheets. Set on the floor was a Decauville type narrow gauge railway system complete with points and turntables to allow entry into any of the buildings (see illustration on page 15). According to the official history, 12 boxes or six kegs were taken from an expense store, loaded on a truck and moved to one of the sifting houses on the unit. Here the picric acid would be sifted to remove any lumps before being loaded into cans in which the acid was to be melted, reloaded on to a truck and delivered to one of the melt houses.

Each of the two units, set between its empty shell store and its transit shed, consisted of eight melt houses in blocks of four surrounded by 22 filling houses. The melt cans were made either of copper or aluminium and came in two sizes, containing either 25 or 50lb but the smaller were preferred because they were easier to handle and resulted in fewer spillages. Once emptied, the boxes that had contained the lyddite were taken to a box store sited on the edge of the unit.

In the melt house the cans were placed in an oil tank which was heated by the producer gas plant. Temperatures were very strictly controlled, that of the acid never being allowed to exceed 141°C – the melting point of picric acid is 133°C – for reasons of safety, and a temperature controller responsible only to the factory manager was appointed to monitor the process. Once the acid was fully melted, the cans were lidded and taken to the filling houses. Each house was, again, as with the bond store cubicles, allowed to hold no more than 3,000lb of explosive. Empty shells were arranged in double rows to ease filling. The shell was filled in layers to a specific depth and, to ensure the acid was properly solidified, a precise time interval was specified before the next layer of explosive was added. Filling was a two-woman operation, with one pouring and the other measuring the distance between the open top of the shell and the top level of the explosive. As the lyddite cooled, the crust was carefully broken to prevent the formation of cavities, and there were rules detailing the essential actions which had to be taken if anything went wrong. Once the final fill had been added, a former was inserted into the top layer of liquid lyddite to produce a cylindrical cavity into which the more sensitive exploder was to be fitted. A thin layer of either kit (beeswax) or liquid TNT was added to seal off the exploder from the lyddite, and once this had set the exploder was inserted and compressed. The shell was sealed by fitting the nose plug and it was then removed to the transit shed.

Cans were only used twice before they were sent to the wash house for cleaning. Here the acid in the can was covered with water and washing soda was added before the can was heated by steam to a maximum of 70°C—above this figure the metal of the can could be attacked by the combination of washing soda and picric acid. Any over-filled or otherwise defective shells were treated in exactly the same way to remove the picric acid from their interior.

After filling began at Rotherwas, output rose only gradually in the first three months of operation due mainly to the inexperience of the workforce. A number of potential supervisors were therefore sent to Banbury for training, and on their return output rose, as Table 1 shows.

Compressing exploders on the left and pouring acid on the right. The girl on the right is pouring liquid lyddite with her companion standing ready to measure with a gauge the depth to which the shell has been filled. Those working in the lyddite section wore light coloured clothing, in the amatol area it was dark. Through the gap on the left, the side walls of the roofed corridor can be seen (PRO MUN 5/185/26)

A very posed photograph showing the four parts of the finishing process, these being, from left to right: repairing, kitting, formering and breaking-down. Note the protective covers over the shells in the first two parts to prevent the outside of the shell case being contaminated (PRO MUN 5/185/26)

Date	Calibre	No. produced	Total	No. per employee
11/11/16 to 11/12/16	6 inch (15 cm)	2,166	2,166	10.88
12/12/16 to 11/1/17	6 inch (15 cm)	9,166		30.71
	8 inch (20 cm)	1,460	10,626	
12/1/17 to 11/2/17	6 inch (15 cm)	23,907	24,775	40.03
	9 inch type IX (22.5 cm)	868		
	9 inch type II	88	24,863	
12/2/17/ to 11/3/17	6 inch (15 cm)	24,785		45.47
	8 inch (20 cm)	29,580		
	9.2 inch (23 cm)	103	54,468	

Table 1 Monthly output figures for Unit 1 of the lyddite section for the first four months of operation, after which Unit 2 joined production

The total output of lyddite filled shells produced at Rotherwas during the war comprised 1,238,680 shells of 6 inch calibre, 127,582 shells of 8 inch calibre and 23,636 shells of 9.2 inch calibre and a limited number of 9 inch calibre shells. In all 8,903.56 tons of picric acid was used.[2]

As more amatol became available the use of picric acid was gradually run down and the lyddite section was closed on 13 April 1918. Because of a huge explosion at the Chillwell factory and a consequent shortage of shells, Unit 2 of the section was reactivated on 3 August 1918 and continued to fill shells until the end of the war. Unit 1 was converted to charge shells with mustard gas as from October 1918.[3]

The Amatol Section[4]

The six redesigned units to handle 80/20 amatol were grouped into three pairs, each with an ammonium nitrate store, an ammonium nitrate dryer, a TNT expense store, an incorporation house and pressing/filling facilities. The ammonium nitrate stores and the TNT bond stores (magazines) were sited as far as possible from each other, respectively on the southern and northern edges of the section.

The ammonium nitrate was at first supplied in casks, but later was delivered in bulk from a new factory at Swindon. Before use, it was dried down to a moisture content of 0.4% and then placed into round covered tins containing 40lb of product and taken to the incorporation house. These buildings were set midway between the ammonium nitrate driers and the TNT expense stores.

TNT was delivered to the TNT bond stores (the TNT magazines) packed in linen bags and placed in wooden boxes which each contained 50lb of explosive. Each store was limited to a capacity of 100 tons of TNT and were, besides being distanced from the main part of the section and each other, surrounded by earth traverses intended to direct the force of any explosion upwards and away from adjacent stores. When required, the boxes were delivered by train to the storage compartment of the expense store on the northern edge of the section. Removed to the working compartment, the TNT was weighed out into tins each containing 10lb and taken to the incorporation house as required. The empty boxes and bags were removed to be stored in the nearby box store.

Incorporation was done using edge runner mills similar to the machines used for gunpowder manufacture – they resemble cider mills but have twin rollers. The edge mills weighed 25cwt were under-driven at 10 rpm. 120lb of ammonium nitrate and 30lbs of TNT were placed in the mill, which was then run for 20 minutes. The amatol so produced was loaded into covered tins, each containing 75lb. The capacity of the incorporation mills in the unit was such that the section could produce 17,000lb of amatol each hour. Amatol which was to be mechanically filled was then taken to the crusher to ensure freedom from lumps which could interfere with the working of the extruder machines. For the preliminary charges and when hand stemming was employed, crushing was unnecessary. Smoke mixture, added to a shell to make it easier to observe exactly where it had landed, was prepared in a similar way to amatol but with had ammonium chloride added to the mix.

In the filling process itself the first item to be put in place was the smoke mixture where a weighed amount was added loose or in bags to the base of the shell. For hand stemming a weighed quantity of amatol, between 80 and 87% of the total, was poured into the shell using a funnel to avoid spillage. The amatol, in appearance similar to soap flakes, had to be compacted and this could be done either by machine or by hand stemming.[5] Hand stemming used a stick similar to a broom handle, inserting it into the shell to rest on the explosive and then hitting it with a wooden mallet. Hand stemming was all but the standard method of filling in both the First and Second World Wars; shown a picture of the tools used in filling shells with amatol in the First War, a Second World War worker immediately recognised the wooden sticks used to stem munitions.[6]

Mechanical filling employed a vertical screw auger within a tube which was fed from a hopper above. The shell was placed on a wheeled bogie and positioned so that when it was raised, the auger and tube entered it. An automatic trip activated the auger

Two incorporation mills with girls removing amatol. The First World War saw many injuries and deaths from TNT poisoning – toxic jaundice. The total absence of any protective clothing, even masks and gloves, suggests that this picture was taken soon after the amatol section became operational and before the way TNT poisoning occurred was fully understood. Note the heavy blast door on the right which could be used to isolate the area (PRO MUN 5.186/1340/31)

which began to deliver amatol. As more amatol was fed into the shell, the resistance encountered increased and was balanced against an appropriate set of weights which allowed the shell to be lowered as it filled. The balancing method used meant that it was unnecessary to weigh the charge.

After each filling/stemming, the shell was moved away and an intermediate charge was put in and hand stemmed, before it was positioned under an hydraulic press to compress the amatol. The process of filling and compaction was repeated, with the number of pressings varying, according to the weight of the charge as per the table below:

Weight	No of pressings
45lb	4
32lb	3
16lb	2

Table 2 The number of pressings in relation to the weight of the charge

With shells coming from a wide range of manufacturers including imports, the internal capacities of the shells in any given batch often varied from that laid down in the engineering specification and it was found necessary to calibrate ten shells from each delivery. This was done by filling them with water to arrive at the volume of the cavity within the shell, allowing the appropriate charge to be calculated to give the required density. Filling was completed by plugging which involved pouring in molten TNT to form a cavity for the exploder. Where the exploder was in a paper tube, a metal former was used and removed once the TNT had set.

Exploders were at first compressed in the shell but following an explosion at another factory, compression was done in a special container, as a separate operation.

After plugging, the shell was taken to the transit shed where it was would be weighed and stamped with the weight group into it fell. When fired, shells of differing weights using a standard propellant charge will travel differing distances, so the volume of propellant has to be adjusted to the weight of the shell. At the point of weighing, each shell was examined by an inspector independent of the factory, trained and employed by Woolwich Arsenal; by August 1916 Woolwich had trained 30,000 such inspectors of whom 14,000 were women.[7] Once weighed and passed, the nose of the shell would be fitted with a grummet – a length of rope which allowed it to be mechanically lifted – and stencilled.

Development of new tools was encouraged by the management of the National Factories, the inventor receiving a royalty, and a grummetting machine was developed at Rotherwas. But this led to its own problems. The deputy managing director of the factory, Mr. Stokes, was accused in January 1918 by the manager of the amatol section of insisting that orders for this grummetting tool should be placed with a firm who were paying Mr. Stokes a royalty. The charges, however, were dismissed.[8]

The war also saw rapid development of measuring gauges, which allowed unskilled workers to accurately measure tolerances. These proved a vitally important part of the expansion of the munitions industry, allowing women to take the place of skilled men who could then be released to serve in the armed forces. Indeed, a National Factory making nothing but gauges was established by the Ministry of Munitions.[9]

Hot Filling with Amatol

When the new 80/20 amatol mix was introduced, the building of Unit 1 was too far advanced to allow the change to 'press' filling accomplished in the other six units. After serving as a hostel for the workers engaged in building the factory, it was converted into an experimental hot-fill unit for 80/20 amatol. The experiments only began to be successful in the early part of 1918, meaning that this unit was never fully operational. The first shells were filled in March 1918 but the main plant was only brought into operation just before the armistice was signed in November 1918. Selected outputs from this hot fill unit were as follows.

Week ending	60 pdr	6 inch
29 April 1918	-	2,726
15 July 1918	12,769	-
7 September 1918	16,483	-
8 November 1918	20,401	-

Table 3 The way output from the hot fill unit built up as experience in this new method of filling was obtained

In the hot-fill method the ammonium nitrate was first dried and crushed, before being placed in a mixer, where it was pre-heated. The pre-heaters consisted of steam jacketed cylinders holding a charge of 800lb. The hot ammonium nitrate, at 95°C, was moved to a kettle where 350lb was incorporated with the requisite amount of TNT. The process took 20 to 30 minutes. The hot amatol, at between 85 and 90°C, was emptied onto a series of covered vessels on an endless rope and delivered into the hopper of a horizontal screw filling machine. The hopper was provided with a steam jacket. The horizontal filler worked on the same principle as the vertical one used in the cold 'press' process but filled at over twice the rate – 20lb as opposed to 9lb. Adjustment to suit differing sizes of shells was also easier.

The hot filling process developed at Rotherwas during the First World War was generally adopted in the 1930s as a standard method of filling shells. Not only was it a much faster process than cold filling, but the machinery employed was also less costly.

Charging Shells with Mustard Gas[10]

The Official History states that gas charging at Rotherwas began in the week ending 11 October 1918 but another document states that on 13 August 1918 the gas charging unit at Rotherwas was asked to accept 500,000 gas shells originally manufactured for the Russians, but not delivered before the revolution that ended that country's participation in the war. The shells were first to be ground down to fit French 75mm guns which had been supplied to the American forces in France. A letter dated 4 September and addressed to the managing director of the factory stated that these shells would be arriving in about six weeks time, but there is no record of this actually happening.[11]

Gas shells were charged in part of Unit 1 of the lyddite section that had closed in April 1918. Four of the filling houses were equipped with two gas charging machines – a total of eight in all – which were designed to deliver a measured quantity of liquid mustard gas into a special gas shell. Four of the melt houses were used as bond stores where charged shells were held for 48 hours to check for possible leaks. Two other filling houses were converted to cater for the filling of the burster charge with fumyl, a mixture of TNT, ammonium chloride and ammonium nitrate, and the exploder, and two more were used to hold supplies of mustard gas.[12]

Empty shells – both steel and cast iron were used – were delivered to the shell store and as with lyddite filling, they were first cleaned before being passed over the dirty/clean barrier for painting and storage until required. Unlike the other combatants in the First World War, the British delivered the gas into the shell through a charging hole in the side rather than from the top. This made for easier manufacture of the shell where the open top could be machined to provide a thread into which a separate sealed container which would later be filled with explosive could be screwed. However, it proved less easy to obtain an accurate measurement of the volume of gas within the shell rather than when charging was done from the top.

Mustard gas was delivered to Hereford in drums which were brought to a lean-to shed attached to the charging house and connected by pipeline to the charging machines. The statement in both the Halcrow (January 1994) and Giffard (April 2000) reports for Herefordshire Council, that mustard gas was manufactured at the Kenchester Chemical Works north of Hereford, is incorrect. The Pontithel Chemical Works at Kenchester is listed in Kelly's *Directory* in both 1913 and 1929. In 2001 there was still evidence of a railside site with decaying corrugated iron buildings, but a luxuriant growth of nettles indicated a 19th-century high fertility site where superphosphate had been produced using bones and sulphuric acid, not by any means a by-product of mustard gas production. The records from the National Archives contain extensive details of just how difficult it was to produce usable volumes of mustard gas and record the sites where the gas was produced during the First World War. They do not mention Kenchester.

For charging with mustard gas the empty shell was laid on its side and a temporary lead plug punched into the shell. The shell was then rotated and if any moisture appeared at the plug hole it would be rejected. It was then placed onto a conveyor where one

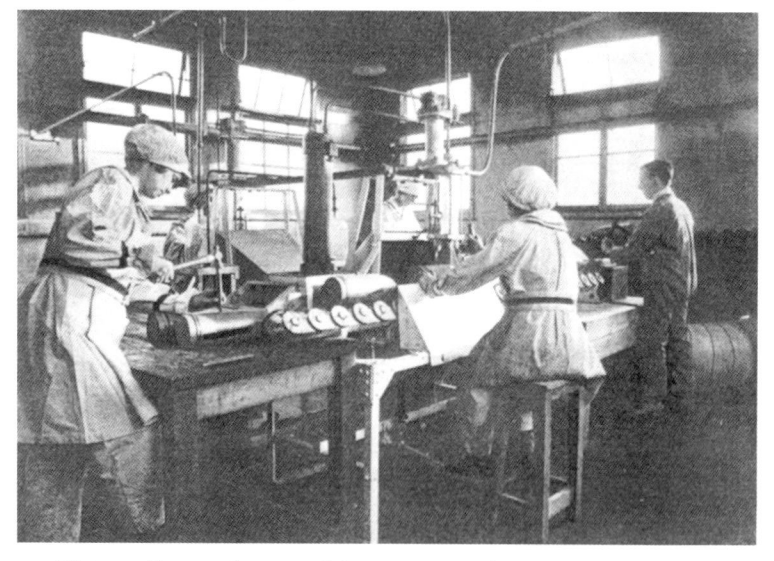

This well posed view of the interior of one of the charging houses at Hereford seems to show a drum of gas actually in the corner of the house. There are wooden benches and a stool, which were to prove capable of absorbing mustard gas. The man to the right wears no protective clothing. The girls wear exactly the same clothing as did those filling shells with lyddite
(PRO SUPP 6/622)

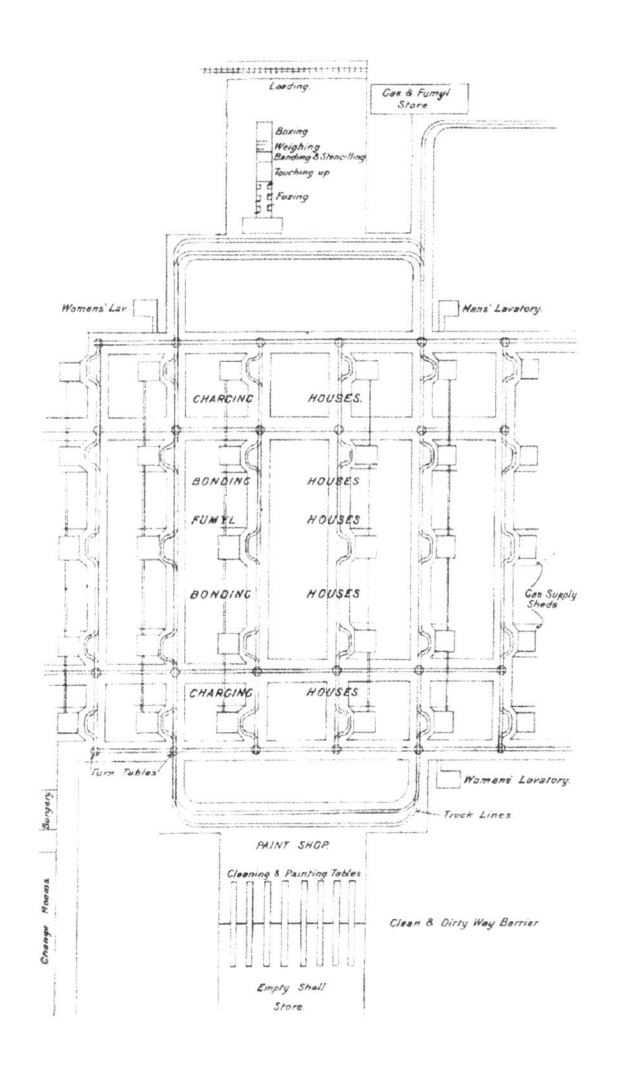

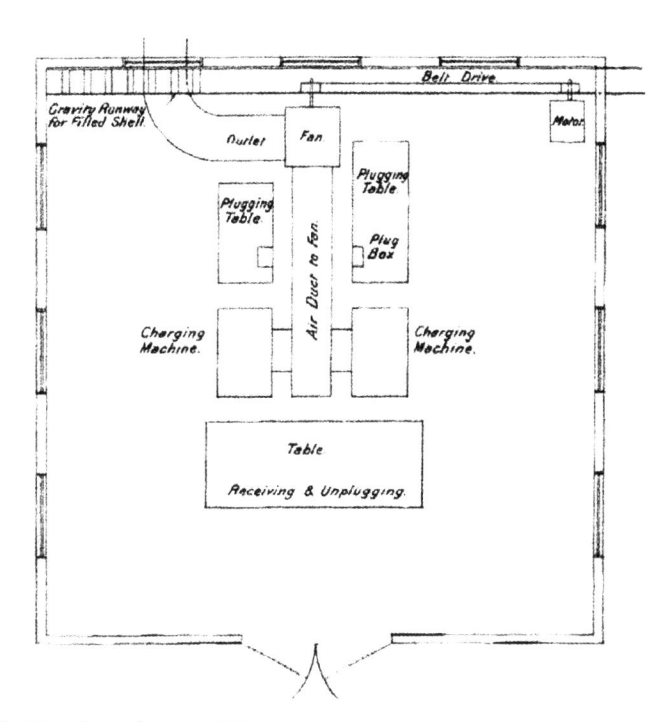

Left: The four former filling houses which were converted late in the war for charging mustard gas shells. Hereford was the third and last place to be used to charge munitions with mustard gas and lessons learnt at Chittering and Banbury were applied (PRO SUPP 6.662)

Above: The layout of one of the charging houses at Rotherwas. The charging machines delivered a measured volume of the liquid gas into the shell with the fan drawing air away along the ducting (PRO SUPP 6.662)

of the two people charging shells first selected a suitably sized iron plug – the bung holes varied in diameter and a selection of plugs of differing sizes was available! The shell was then positioned beneath the nozzle supplying the gas and raised using a foot pedal, to allow the nozzle which was to supply the liquid to enter the body of the shell via the bung hole. A chain was pulled which delivered a measured volume of gas into the shell. Pulling the chain further opened a valve and allowed a vacuum to draw on the surface of the charge thus removing any surplus and ensuring that the hopper was emptied. A second pull at the chain sucked up any drips. The operator then *carefully* – the word is emphasised on posters – inserted the steel plug and moved the shell along the conveyor to where another operator sealed the shell by hammering home the iron plug to produce a 0.15 inch depression. This was further sealed using a hammered-home lead seal.

The charged shell was then delivered to the bond store. Here the shells were first stencilled with the date of charging and then stored plug down for 48 hours to check for leaks. Passing this test, the shell was taken to the transit shed for filling with the exploder. For a 4.5 inch shell the burster charge of 6oz of fumyl was put in place and hand stemmed. An exploder was then fitted and the shell sealed with liquid TNT before being fuzed. The final operation before grummetting and boxing was to paint a series of coloured bands identifying the shell as containing mustard gas and its weight group.[13]

With hindsight, it is easy to criticise the working methods adopted to charge munitions with mustard gas. G.S. Whitman, a chemical engineer in the department of the Master General of Ordnance, wrote in March 1927 that gas charging in the First World War had incurred high casualties prompting great difficulty in obtaining new labour. Between 21 June and 7 December 1918 the factory at Avonmouth recorded 1,213 casualties – a term that indicated a worker was off work for more than three days.[14] Numerous casualties during the opening of drums were incurred at Banbury where charging began in mid-summer 1918.[15]

It was later realized that many of the working surfaces in the charging houses actually absorbed mustard gas. The conveyor delivering shells to the bond store had wooden rollers, whilst the floor was of asphalt. Shoes were a particular problem as they absorbed gas over a period without the operators being aware of the contamination until ulcerous blisters appeared on their feet.[16]

The facilities at Rotherwas for charging munitions with gas were kept in place during the 1920s and may even have been extended. These developments are described in chapter 6.

	18 pdr	4.5 inch	Total
W/e 11 October 1918	25	25	50
18 October	730	348	1,078
25 October	242	1,740	1,982
1 November		711	711

Table 5 Numbers of shells charged with mustard gas in Unit 1 of the Northern Section at Rotherwas

Table 5 shows a total of 3,796 mustard gas shells charged at Rotherwas, but as with all the filling factories, no production returns were made for the week ending Friday 8 November 1918, and it is likely that charging continued during that week as did filling on the Southern Section.[17]

4 Labour in the First World War

During the First World War there was no compulsory direction of labour into the munitions industry either for men or women, although once employed in any job in munitions men could not obtain a new job without producing an official leaving certificate obtained from their previous employer. Even here the onus was on the employer rather than the employee, for it was the employer who had to refuse to employ any male unable to produce a certificate. Women were attracted into munitions only by appeals to their patriotic feelings and by the lure of high wages; they could leave whenever they wanted.

Both males and females employed in National Factories were given badges inscribed 'On War Service', allowing them to display the fact that they were serving their country even if they were not wearing uniform.[1] Males in civilian clothes, particularly in 1915/16, were likely to be presented with a white feather and accused of cowardice.

Early in the war the government opened a register of women willing to work in munitions but it was left to Lloyd George, after his appointment as Minister of Munitions and prompted by the king, to reach an agreement with the Women's Social and Political Union to encourage more women to join the workforce. In March 1915 the government reached what was known as the Dilution Agreement with the Union, under which women would be encouraged to take up work in return for the promise of votes after the war. The Agreement also stressed that the employment of unskilled men or women was only for the duration of the war, and that men in the armed services would get their jobs back in peace time. (It was certainly the case that it was only in some areas of employment where women had replaced men that they continued to be employed once the war ended and demobilisation began). Within 12 months 264,000 women had registered as being willing to undertake some form of war work.[2]

In the opening few weeks of the war many women who had been employed in the luxury trades were sacked. High levels of unemployment were quickly evident in such areas as the London dressmaking businesses. In September 1914 one estimate suggested that 44.4% of the female workforce were unemployed.[3]

As a result, the Ministry of Labour divided the country into two types of districts: those where there was surplus labour, and those where there was a demand for munition workers beyond that which the district could supply. Recruitment was the responsibility of the Labour Exchanges and they ran a National Clearing House intended to match vacancies with recruits. Every Exchange appointed a women officer and supported her with women clerks. A weekly newspaper was produced listing vacancies and this was sent to all the women's departments of the Labour Exchanges. Officers at an exchange sending workers to a munitions factory were responsible for helping to arrange transport to their destination, and some areas where there was a surplus of labour arranged recruitment meetings.

As the building of the National Factories was completed, more and more workers were needed and in the last three months of

1916 the number of women who moved to work in factories outside their local area rose to between 14,000 and 15,000. The system worked well until early in 1917, and although it continued to operate the numbers of workers required became too great for it to cope. In all the numbers placed in the various munitions workplaces during the war was 1,035,747;[4] by 1918 one in every 20 women in the UK was working in munitions.[5]

The Labour Exchange at Hereford was entirely responsible for recruiting and 'importing' workers for Rotherwas, subject to the conditions placed on them by the factory management. A female worker expressing an interest in coming to work at Hereford was given instructions as to how to get there but had to make her own way to the city, paying her own fare. On arrival she would first be directed to the Labour Exchange where she would present her identification from the Labour Exchange in the district she had left. The Hereford Labour Exchange would then issue a Green Card and from June 1917 pass her on to the factory nurse who examined her for cleanliness. Any of the women found to be verminous – and many were – were referred to the Clearing Hostel for cleaning.[6] In any event, new arrivals spent their first night there. Here they were charged 2s. 6d. to cover supper, lodgings, breakfast, and lunch at the factory. This payment was very unpopular and the food was described as inadequate.[7] The Hereford Clearing Hostel, established in June 1917, was run by the House and Grounds Sub-Committee of the City Council, itself responsible to the Housing Sub-Committee which in turn reported to a government appointed body, the Herefordshire Advisory Committee for Women's War Employment, Industrial.

In the morning the women had to make their own way to the factory – usually they walked – where they were first interviewed by the Lady Superintendent, passed on to the doctor for a medical, checked as to *bona fides* by the factory police and then allocated to a particular job. Once back at the hostel on the completion of their first day's work, they were sent to their lodgings. These arrangements were severely criticised by the Ministry's Committee of Enquiry (see page 38) who suggested that the first week's lodgings should be free.[8]

It would appear that whilst Belgian refugees were employed in several of the country's National Factories,[9] this was not the case in Hereford despite the fact that the city was the first town in Britain to offer sanctuary to them – the first arrived on 23 September 1914. No record of any taking up work at Rotherwas has been found even though the refugees remained in the city until March 1919.[10]

Likewise, it has not been possible to find exactly where labour employed at Rotherwas was recruited. Surveys of the labour forces at other munitions factories show that roughly a third of the workforce had previously been employed in domestic service, whilst many others had been living at home with no job outside household duties. Smaller numbers had worked as shop assistants, farmworkers, laundry women, dressmakers, schoolteachers or clerks.[11] As the war progressed, an ever greater proportion came from other munitions factories or other forms of factory work. In the main those employed at Rotherwas because of the heavy nature of the work, were, as with other filling factories, most likely to have been working in some form of labouring job and were attracted to work in munitions by the relatively high wages paid.

Occasionally in a report of the magistrates court there is mention of the place of origin of a defendant charged with possession of prohibited substances. From these records it can be deduced that women came to work at Rotherwas from Barry, Porthcawl, Pembrokeshire, the Welsh Valleys, North Shropshire, Staffordshire, Manchester and southern Ireland.[12]

The Ministry of Munitions began to collect statistics regarding the numbers employed at each National Factory as from 15 September 1916. These returns listed the numbers employed on the third Friday of each month until the end of the war.[13] Employment at Rotherwas during the war reached its peak in the week ending Saturday 14 September 1918 when a return listing 5,760 employees was made by the Ministry of Munitions in a separate record.[13] Of these, 3,917 (68%) were females, women or youths under the age of military call up.[14] After this date numbers began to fall. In all, around 16,000 people were employed at Rotherwas during the two years from November 1916 to November 1918, suggesting that 'wastage' was a considerable problem with many workers finding conditions not to their liking and soon leaving.[15]

The returns for Rotherwas are reproduced in Table 6. The figures between December 1917 and November 1918 show an unexplained increase in male employees of 1,000, the number doubling in the 12 months. No explanation for this increase has been found and it is not mirrored at other National Filling Factories, where numbers of male employees generally

Date	Total Employed	Total Women	Total Men	% Women
Nov. 1916	199	142	57	
Dec.	346	262	84	71.4
Jan. 1917	619	467	152	75.4
Feb.	1,154	819	355	71
Mar.	1,559	1,161	398	74.5
Apr.	1,630	1,198	434	73.5
May	1,843	1,355	488	73.5
Jun.	1,935	1,413	522	73
Jul.	2,191	1,588	603	72.5
Aug.	2,741	2,130	617	77.7
Sep.	3,482	2,786	686	80
Oct.	3,548	2,948	600	83.1
Nov.	3,741	2,907	834	77.7
Dec.	4,205	3,217	988	76.5
Jan. 1918	4,668	3,501	1,167	75
Feb.	4,813	3,605	1,208	74.9
Mar.	4,473	3,265	1,208	73
Apr.	3,858	2,724	1,134	70.6
May	3,613	2,493	1,120	69
Jun.	4,224	2,893	1,331	68.5
Jul.	4,884	3,419	1,565	68.6
Aug.	5,560	3,792	1,768	68.2
Sep.	5,760	3,917	1,843	68
Oct.	5,864	3,982	1,882	67.9
Nov.	5,512	3,578	1,934	64.9

Table 6 The table shows the number employed at Rotherwas with the figures taken from the monthly return the factory made to the Ministry of Munitions

decrease in this period as the demands for fighting men in France escalated. Hereford ranked sixth of the National Filling Factories in terms of the numbers employed. Georgetown (Renfrewshire) topped the list with 13,188 employees in April 1917, second came Aintree (Liverpool) with 12,658 employees in August 1917, followed by Hayes (Middlesex) with 11,379 employees in April 1917. Chillwell (Nottingham) was fourth with 9,194 employees in August 1917, Quedgley (Gloucester) fifth with 6,415 employees in July 1918. Very similar to Rotherwas in terms of employment was Perivale (Middlesex) with 5,241 employees in March/April 1917.[16] Of these only Chilwell was producing a similar product – breech loading shells.

Hereford was not a popular factory because of its situation and the nature of the work done. Its inability to attract sufficient labour became the subject in July 1918 of the only inquiry into labour shortages at any of the First World War filling factories.[17]

The Committee of Inquiry into the Shortage of Labour
In July 1918 the Ministry of Munitions set up a committee to 'Inquire into the Causes of Insufficient Labour Supply and Wastage at the Hereford National Filling Factory'. They only spent two days in Hereford, yet produced a report which was a scathing condemnation of those involved in managing the workforce in and out of the factory.

The report provides details regarding employment at Rotherwas, as shown in Table 7.

Department	Men	Women
Office	89	100
Amatol Section	967	2,642
Stores	137	-
Picric Acid Section	45	92
Nurses	-	12
General Stores	17	15
Canteen	3	108
Traffic	35	-
Police	91	44
Engineers	313	-
Total	1,697	3,013

Table 7 Numbers employed in various departments on 18 July 1918

The total of 4,710 workers compares with the official return made to the Ministry of Munitions the following day of 4,948. The committee were told that there was a need for a further 1,797 workers to fully man the factory – 517 women and 260 men for the amatol section, and 670 women and 350 men for the lyddite section. The latter figure may have reflected the proposed reopening of Unit 2 of the lyddite section which had been shut down on 13 April 1918 and was to be reactivated on 3 August 1918.[18] At the time of the visit just days before this reopening, only 137 people, all male, were employed there.

Intriguingly, the report notes that on 4 May 1918 an increase in the workforce had been made necessary by a demand for filling bombs. This is the only mention of bomb filling at any filling factory, but the First World War saw the beginning of bombing with the development in the last few weeks of the war of allied aircraft capable of reaching Berlin.

Miss Lillian Baker (on the left) with a group of women workers at Woolwich Arsenal. She was in charge of all the women working there. Miss Baker was a member of the Committee of Inquiry into the Shortage of Labour at Rotherwas and almost certainly the author of much of their very critical report. She went on to become the first ever female prison governor and was awarded an OBE for her services during the war (IWM Q27889)

The committee was told that between 4 May and 26 July the Labour Exchange had supplied the factory with 1,696 women, of whom only 351 were local, mainly as replacements for those leaving. Staff turnover was high, with as many as 4% of the total workforce leaving in a single week. The number of workers leaving was supposed to be notified to the local Labour Exchange so that these could be included in the national Clearing House figures, but Rotherwas had failed to make any returns between 2 March and 16 April 1918.

Additional to workers leaving was the problem of absenteeism. One witness appearing before the committee suggested that this had been as high as 430 people failing to turn up on a single occasion, a rate approaching 10% of the workforce.

The committee spent time visiting the various parts of the factory and listed faults for most of the operations, suggesting that the work was extremely hard and few labour saving devices were available. A major criticism was that insufficient ventilation was provided. The Health of Munitions Workers Committee appointed by the Ministry of Munitions late in 1915 had reported on 'Ventilation and Lighting of Workshops' in January 1916, well before the buildings at Rotherwas were planned or erected and the guidelines they laid down should have been followed.[19]

Other points where the committee found fault included the lack of provision of rest rooms and of a surgery. An interview with Mrs. Eastwood of the factory welfare staff raised the problem of fatigue resulting from menstruation. Rotherwas had not followed the action of many other National Filling Factories in allowing women a day's paid leave every month.

The report also shows high turnover among the management. Eleven members of the management team had left in the previous six months and the Lady Superintendent and her three assistants had resigned on 1 July. The committee were unable to find the reason for these resignations but felt that it was as a result of strong personality clashes with the senior management. To replace the Lady Superintendent, the Assistant Secretary to the factory, a Mrs. Harding, had been appointed and her only permanent help was Mrs. Dunnett, the wife of the secretary. One of the committee's recommendations was that the appointments of Mrs. Harding and Mrs. Dunnett should not be confirmed. Additionally they uncovered poor relations between several other management branches but a major row erupted when Miss Lillian Baker, a member of the committee, witnessed the arrival of 65 new women workers at the factory. They had walked from the Labour Exchange during a heavy thunderstorm and arrived soaked. Miss Baker drew this to Mr. Dunnett's attention, as secretary to the factory, and asked that their clothing should be dried. The report states: 'somewhat to our surprise he first denied that the women were wet and then went on to state that the factory had no means of drying their clothes'. Miss Baker insisted on drying but Mr. Dunnett stated that the case was quite exceptional as 'no rain had fallen in Hereford since February'!

Rules of Employment
In October 1917 when the first case against a worker of possessing matches and smoking materials in a secure area was heard, the local magistrates asked for someone from the factory to appear to make clear how rules against prohibited articles were explained to those taken on as workers. Colonel Knox-Gore told the court that a rule book entitled *Rules for Employees of the Ammunition Filling Factories not including the Royal Factories*[20] was handed to each person by the staff superintendent with the admonition to make themselves fully conversant with it. He would then obtain a written receipt for the book. Later the Lady Superintendent would explain the rules fully and the dangers against which they were designed to guard. As this was the first case regarding possession of matches and smoking material the magistrates warned the offenders, but later one month's imprisonment became the norm for possession of matches with a £5 fine for those found with a cigarette. The local papers carried regular reports of several convictions every time the magistrates sat.[21] The eight-page rules booklet was printed on stiff card and was designed so that it could be carried in a pocket.

Wages
The cost of living rose during the war but so did the overall level of wages, largely because people worked longer hours. With some exceptions, the working classes enjoyed an improving standard of living. Juveniles over 14 did particularly well and could earn between £1 and £2 a week in munition factories. Indeed it was often the money earned by the children which lifted the living standard of the family.[22] Wages in the munition factories tended to be higher than in other industries as was recalled in 1937 in the *Hereford Times* when a retired railway inspector recorded his memories. He was still most resentful of what he saw

as the high wages paid to the women working in munitions. 'During World War One', he told the reporter, 'long serving railway workers were being paid £1 15s., [per week] while my daughter was earning between £3 and £4 at Rotherwas'.[23]

Life was tough for women left behind by those serving in the forces, particularly in the early years of the war, and was a major reason why many sought work in munition factories. Pensions for the widows of servicemen were not introduced until November 1915 and then only at the rate of 7s. 6d. per week for the widow of a private.[24]

Accommodation and Welfare
The majority of non-locals coming to work at Rotherwas were accommodated in lodgings. In evidence given to the Committee of Inquiry in July 1918 the shortage of lodging was cited as one considerable difficulty in attracting and keeping labour. By then 2,100 workers were billeted in Hereford and 310 in Ross. The factory authorities suggested that a further 300 could be housed in Hereford and 100 in Ross, with Leominster, where special trains were due to start running, soon being able to find accommodation for another 500. Later in the war women were found lodgings even further away in Presteigne,[25] and there were plans to start to enlist householders in Ledbury and Ludlow where 400 to 500 billets in each town might be available.

The Board of Guardians for the Hereford Workhouse were informed in March 1917 that the Ministry of Munitions was considering taking over their building as a hostel for women workers.[26] The Union Workhouse had accommodation for 300 inmates and there had been a suggestion in July 1916 to take over the workhouse as accommodation for those building the factory, but as with the later proposal it was not followed through.[27] In the event, the Ministry acquired Castle Pool House, a building that now houses Hereford's most prestigious and expensive hotel.[28]

The Billeting Act was brought into force in Hereford and Leominster during the early part of 1917, but no attempt to enforce the provision that householders with surplus accommodation could be forced to take in lodgers seems to have been made until 1918. Formed in 1917, the Billeting Committee of Hereford Council recorded that Hereford had provided billets for 3,221 women and 662 men, and that Leominster had made 360 and Ross 556 places available.[29]

The Billeting Committee published the official charges for various types of lodgings depending upon how many shared a bedroom, and set out the services that landladies would provide. For those working the day shift these included a cup of tea, cocoa or coffee with bread and butter before starting out for work, a hot meal, including meat, on return from work and dinner on Saturdays and full meals on Sundays. For those working the night shift they had to provide a cup of tea, cocoa, or coffee on rising at around 4 p.m., a hot meal, again including meat, before the women started out for work, a hot breakfast on return from work, dinner on Saturdays and full meals on Sundays and Mondays. In addition all the meals were to be of adequate amounts of wholesome food, but landladies could charge extra for other food supplied and for washing.

In addition to the lodgings, limited numbers of beds were available in hostel accommodation. In Hereford there were three hostels under the control of the Ministry of Munitions and five run by voluntary organisations. The numbers of beds each hostel provided are listed in *Herefordshire in the Great War* and for those controlled by the Ministry of Munitions the actual number of bedsteads sold in the post war disposal sales are available. The figures do not tally. The three ministry controlled hostels were Castle Pool Hostel (Castle Street) providing accommodation for 30 beds but 48 were sold, the Clearing Hostel 37 and 140 respectively and the Highlands Hostel (Broomy Hill) 60 and 110. Included in the sale at the Highlands Hostel were a large number of iron bedsteads from next door, a house owned by the Misses Earl, implying that they were also providing lodgings during the war. The other hostels were the New Womens with 28 beds, the YWCA with 20 beds, Castle Close Board House with 26 and Holly Mount (Girls Friendly Society) with 30.

Hereford was then and remains to some extent even today a rural backwater. It was not a town which could supply much in the way of entertainment but the authorities did their best. A central club was opened in St. Peter's Square on 27 September 1917 and a recreation club at Edgar Street in June 1918.

A National Kitchen opened in the Butter Market on 11 June 1918 being given a gift of 700lb of salmon by the Board of Conservators for the Wye. It extended its opening hours in August mainly for the benefit of the munition workers.[30] No crèche was established at Hereford, unlike at Quedgley the Gloucester filling factory.[31]

Transport

Special trains were run by the GWR from Barrs Court Station to Rotherwas, the Hereford - Ross - Gloucester railway line running through the middle of the factory site. Despite the editorial quoted later stating that rail journeys to the Factory were free, evidence has been found that in March 1918 a weekly workman's return ticket cost 8d.[32] The GWR timetable for July to December 1918 lists two stopping places on its regular service between Hereford and Ross – Rotherwas Junction and Rotherwas South.[33] Map evidence shows that Rotherwas Junction, situated in the Central Section, had two platforms, one for the up and the other for the down line, with a footbridge over the railway connecting them. Another smaller platform lay to the west of the lines which ran through the Central Section and provided access to the Southern Section.[34]

Map evidence also shows that bicycle sheds were provided at each of the three entrances to the clean, secure sections where shells were being filled with explosives – two to the Southern Section and one to the Northern Section.[35] To help those who walked from Hereford, first a ferry was used to take workers across the river from Bartonsham, and later a wooden footbridge was attached to the Eign railway bridge where the line crossed the Wye just north of Rotherwas Junction.[36]

Labour Unrest

During the First World War, much in contrast to the Second World War, there are a number of indications that the factory was badly managed. Mention of labour unrest at the factory is first found in the *Hereford Times* on 9 June 1917, when a report of the deliberations of the Trades Council stated that a strike at Rotherwas had taken place over the way the management had cut wages following the Easter and Whitsun holidays. This had so reduced take-home pay that many women had had to borrow to pay for their lodgings.[37]

According to the Official History of the Rotherwas factory, the Ministry of Munitions introduced a Premium Bonus Scheme in November 1917. Due to the great difficulties in understanding its complex provisions it led to labour unrest,[38] and in evidence given to an inquiry into possible corruption in January 1918 it appears that the Scheme had not yet been implemented. The inquiry also recorded that the various managers did not stay long in post, a factor which would not help in establishing good labour relationships.[39]

TNT Poisoning

The first fatal case of Toxic Jaundice (TNT poisoning) in the munitions industry was reported in February 1915. By December 1916 there had been 86 cases with 23 deaths, and by the end of the war TNT poisoning had accounted for 210 deaths.[40] There were no fatalities after February 1918. The problem was first addressed by the Committee on Special Industrial Diseases appointed in February 1916[41] with a description of the symptoms published in the *Lancet* of 12 August 1916.[42] TNT can enter the body through the skin or be inhaled, and before this was properly understood 'alternation' did much to reduce the problem. From July 1916 women engaged in handling TNT alternated periods of factory work with two or three weeks spent working on the land,[43] a system adopted by all but one of the filling factories by June 1918. At Rotherwas undeveloped land was farmed or used to produce market garden crops, with much of the produce used by the factory canteens.[44] In addition food was banned from the filling areas to ensure that hands were washed before eating, and $1/2$ pint of milk was supplied free of charge each day.

Rotherwas recorded two deaths due to toxic jaundice. One was of a woman who had been employed at the factory and then moved away. The other girl, Maria Lotinga, died in January 1918 having worked at the factory for five months. Her death is recorded in a letter from her sister to the organisers of a Special Service of Remembrance for munition workers who had died, held at St. Paul's Cathedral on 30 April 1918. There is also a report in the *Hereford Journal* on the inquest into her death.[45]

Attitudes to the Workers

The middle and upper classes of the county jumped at the opportunity of imposing their ideals of morals and living conditions onto the women coming to work at the factory. The Clearing House Sub-Committee's attitude to the working women, along with that of other organisations including the factory management, can best be described as well organised snobbery.

The moralistic attitude surfaced in March 1917 in the annual report of the Hereford Rescue Service, established to 'rescue' fallen women. Among the problems they faced they listed 'high wages and excitement' and they deplored 'the behaviour of some women in the city'.[46]

These attitudes, however, were not without some foundation. On 2 August 1917 there was a stand-up fight at Barrs Court Station between Irish and English women. Problems had begun earlier at the factory when an English girl had been accused of taking an Irish woman's dinner. While waiting for the train to take them to the factory the English women on the night shift had accused the Irish of being Sinn Feiners and a fight resulted. The combatants were separated by the station staff and the police, and 20 to 30 Irish women were 'secured' on a staircase until the English women left for the factory by train. The Irish were then released and they marched in procession along Commercial Street to their hostel, carrying banners and shouting 'Ireland for Ever'.

The incident left some serious injuries, with one woman having her arm broken, another was stabbed in the neck with a hat pin and a third was hit over the head with a bottle. The Irish, most of whom lodged at the Judge's Lodging House in Commercial Street, were confined there and between 50 and 60 were sent home the following day.[47] At some later time the factory management banned recruitment of both Irish and Welsh women.[48]

Further trouble was reported in a magistrates court case held in October 1917 when a woman employed at the factory faced a charge of assault. Following the Russian Revolution there was an attempt to organise a strike at Rotherwas, and Barrs Court Station was picketed by two women. On the return of those who had gone into work, Elsie Francis Abel pursued one of them and hit her over the head with the staff on which she'd hung a red flag. She was sentenced to a month's imprisonment. In her defence it was said that the banner was not in fact red but 'rather pinkish'.[49]

Other moralistic efforts grew out of the need for ensuring that workers did not take prohibited materials into the factory, a responsibility that rested with the factory police. There was an obvious difficulty with searching female employees when that force was all male. Women Police Volunteers were first appointed in Grantham in 1914 where the general commanding the 11th Division stationed nearby paid tribute to the two members appointed as a safeguard to the moral welfare of the young women of the town. On 15 February 1915 the Women's Police Service was inaugurated and in April 1916 the Ministry of Munitions asked for women police to be appointed to help at munition factories. The Ministry paid the women and gave them eight weeks training, but they had to purchase their own uniforms.

In Hereford a meeting addressed by Miss Chamney, a member of the Women's Police Service and a native of Llandudno, who for some time had been being looking after the interests of certain workers in the neighbourhood of Hereford, ended with her being created 'Inspector Chamney', and becoming the first member of the Hereford Women's Patrols.[50]

Women's Patrols were an almost entirely volunteer body, though which organisation was responsible for establishing them is unclear, as the sources differ. Some suggest it was the National Union of Women Workers, others the Headmistress Association and the Federation of University Women.[51] From the summer of 1916 their work in the metropolitan areas was subsidised by the police, and they were also employed as park wardens.[52] With stringent middle class ideas of what and what not was seemly, however, they were far from being universally welcomed. A letter to a local paper stated 'that it was about time something was done about ancient spinsters following soldiers about with their flash lights'.[53] Both Women Police and Women's Patrols were the result of an upper and middle class reaction to fears of an outbreak of immorality and were formed 'to save these women from their own folly'.[54] In Hereford they congratulated themselves on their achievements in the following terms: 'Look at the *material* upon which the movement is called to operate and out of which *character* is supposed to be made' (their emphasis).[55] The Women's Patrols began their activities by providing a series of lectures for the women at Rotherwas on the dangers of venereal diseases, and raised the possibility that an excess of alcohol could increase the danger from TNT poisoning.[56] They continued their work locally until the spring of 1919.[57]

As early as January 1917 the *Hereford Journal* and the *Hereford Times* carried the same long leader extolling the efforts of the munitions workers. Using the example of a fictitious filling factory bounded by a famous salmon river, the leader lauded the care with which things were managed to ensure that the amenities of a peaceful countryside were not spoilt, and how the willingness, ability and interest of the women workers in their job had won the hearts of the managers. In an attempt to get more people to volunteer the article went on to enumerate the ideal working conditions the factory offered: the steam laundry, the drying apparatus, the mending room, the provision of free overalls and shoes, and the canteen with its clean electric cookers. It praised the food, with a free breakfast provided to all, and the reporter wrote that he dined to repletion on an 8d. dinner. One reason later advanced as to why the Rotherwas factory failed to attract sufficient labour was that the cost of lodgings and of obtaining food tended to be higher than in other areas.

The article went on to state that the working day was 8.5 hours, with an hour's break for dinner, and that a lady doctor and supervisor were provided. Special trains were run at no expense to the workers to ferry them to and from the factory (as mentioned above, this was probably a false assertion) and the Board of Trade through the Labour Exchange had set up a welfare committee whose duty was to see to the housing, aftercare and recreation of those employed by securing billets and providing clubs. There is a hint, however, of the perception the factory had made amongst the local population, unused to large industrial concerns: 'there has been a tendency to exaggerate its dangers and talk ill-naturedly about its doings'.

The piece finished by urging all women between the ages of 18 and 40 to register for munitions work at the Labour Exchange. There was more on the same lines in articles in both papers the following month.[58]

The Contribution to the War Effort made by Women
The work done by women during the First World War was vital to victory. When war was declared this country was unprepared, its armed forces ill-equipped. For much of the war the development of new weaponry lagged behind that of Germany, but the way in which the forces were backed by a far better mobilisation of the civilian production was perhaps the main difference between the two protagonists.

During the war women took over many previously male dominated jobs: Sidney Pollard in *The Development of the British Economy* states that 800,000 went into engineering, 500,000 were employed in clerical jobs, 250,000 became agricultural labourers and 200,000 took up government jobs. The total number of females employed rose from 3,280,000 in July 1914 to 4,950,000 by November 1918, an increase of 1,670,000. This compares with a loss of male employees of 2,500,000 during the same period. Gerand de Groot in *Blighty. British Society in the Era of the Great War* produces figures one and a half times bigger, stating that the number of women in paid employment increased from 4.93 million to 6.19 million.

In 1914 the number of women in the UK employed in domestic service was 1,658,000. Over the period of the war this fell by 400,000, but even at the end of the war domestic service remained the occupation employing most women. The textile industry slipped from second to third place during the war but in November 1918 still employed more women than did the munitions industry. The biggest increases occurred in banking, finance and commerce who took on an additional 429,000. Middle and upper class women made up only about 9% of the munitions workers and were concentrated in supervisory or skilled jobs. Actual filling work was the lowest of the low. An indication of the place of those employed on this most menial of jobs came from the fact that their skin was stained yellow from contact with TNT or picric acid with the girls nicknamed as canaries. Whilst many lost their jobs at the end of the war, the male clerk and the quill pen had gone for good, with the female typist taking his place.

The contribution made by women led to the passing of the Representation of the Peoples Act which in 1918 for the first time gave votes to 6,000,000 women aged over 30. It was passed by the House of Commons by a majority of 3:1. In 1928 it was extended to all women over 21.

5   November 1918 to September 1939

The signing of the Armistice on 11 November 1918 was swiftly followed by reductions in those employed in the National Factories, particularly amongst the female staff. At Woolwich, well before the provisions of the Dilution Act were applied, about half of the women employed voluntarily withdrew from the labour market, both because they preferred life at home and because they regarded it as a duty to make room for the returning soldiers.[1] On leaving, women workers were given two weeks pay in lieu of notice, a rail pass home and a Certificate of Service. By the end of 1918 it was estimated that 750,000 women had been made redundant and by the end of the following year only 200,000 remained in engineering, up just 20,000 on the pre-war figure. Unemployed women received initial support from the 'Out of Work' donation, a form of unemployment pay which entitled them to £1 for the first 13 weeks and 15 shillings for the second 13 weeks.[2]

Work at Rotherwas stopped around noon on Monday, 11 November 1918 and the rest of the day was declared a holiday. On the Tuesday many employees failed to turn up for work and those that did were so excited that the management decided to shut the factory for a day or two. On Friday 15 November the workers found that they had had not been paid for the days they took off.[3] This led to strong objections and eventually Col. Gaudet, the factory's managing director, agreed to three days paid holiday.[4] The following week he announced that the factory was to be partially closed but that some employees would be kept on. Some 500 workers had already left, a large proportion returning to the cotton mills of Lancashire.[5] Such was the reduction in the workforce that Hereford's Women's Patrols were wound up early in the spring of 1919.[6]

In December 1918 all 16 Army Ordnance Department stores – six at Rotherwas and ten at Credenhill – were handed over to the Central Stores Department (CSD). Major Vincent was appointed to take control of the six stores at Rotherwas, which were renamed CSD No 86. In November 1920 he was to face several charges of embezzlement, it being alleged that he pocketed the money from the sale of hay from the site's farm and from empty shell boxes. He was acquitted on a technicality, in that the prosecution had denied him access to paperwork.[7]

Many munitions sites were released during the 1920s. After the removal of its wooden buildings Banbury was abandoned and remained untouched until the building of the M40 in the 1990s, when the motorway cut through its south-western corner. Some brick structures still survive and it is possible to trace the outlines of many of the other buildings. Much of the site at Gretna was cleared after 1924, but some of the area remained in government ownership and became a Second World War storage depot. National Filling Factory No. 5 at Quedgley (Gloucester) was closed in a piecemeal fashion during the decade and sold off, although it was bought back in 1938 by the Air Ministry as the site for an equipment depot.[8] The National Machine Gun Factory at Burton-upon-Trent became a military storage depot, but in the

47

Plan of the site in 1923

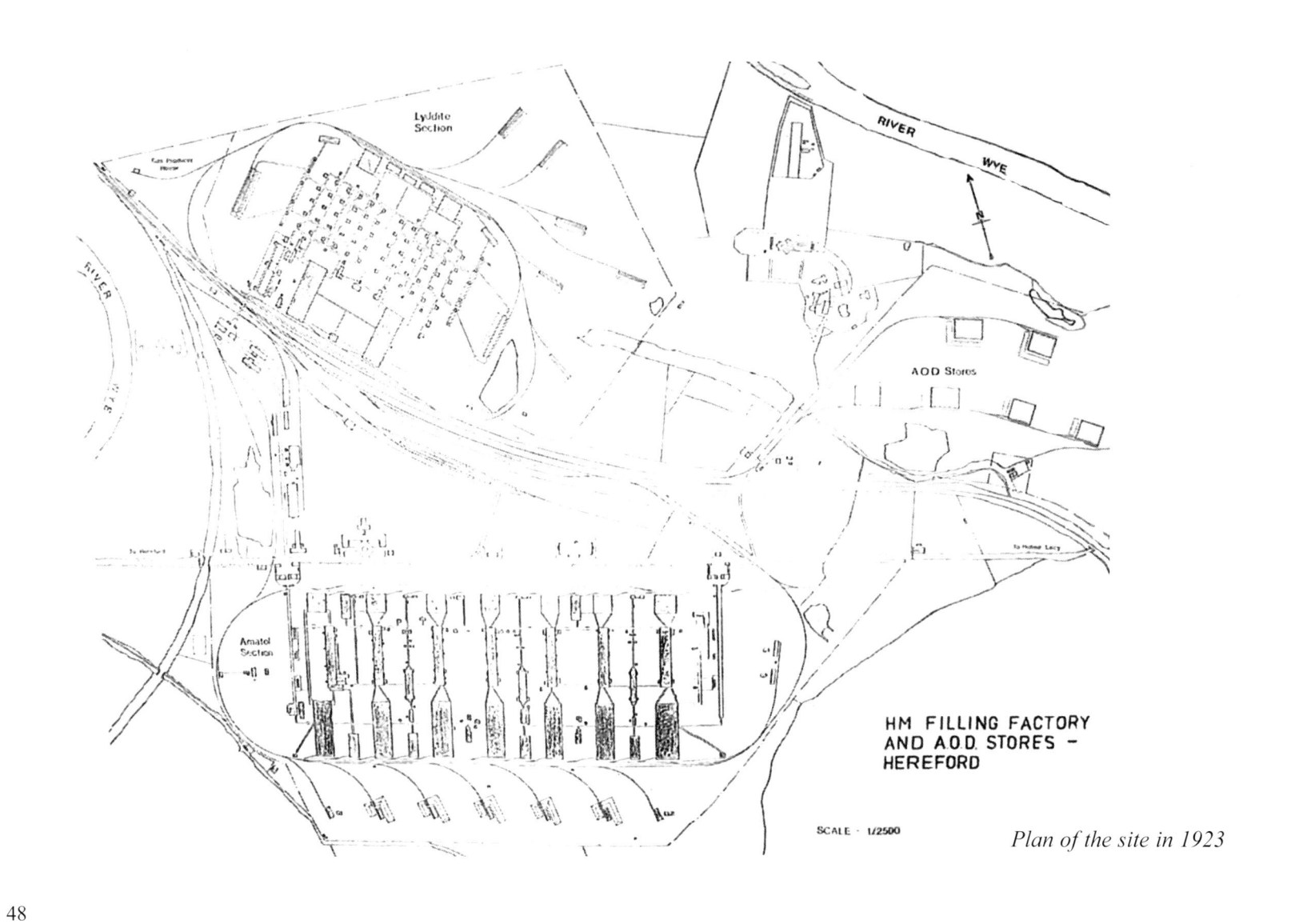

main the munitions factories and military depots were released to civilian use. The buildings which had housed National Filling Factory No. 10 at Coventry became the Swallow car factory and later, when the company changed its name, Jaguars were built there.[9] The numerous London based storage depots became the homes of new industries during the 1920s and 1930s. The 335 acre site of the munitions factory at Perivale (Park Royal) developed into a busy industrial estate, and the prosperity of Slough and the surrounding area owes much to the sale of a military depot established there in 1918.

At Hereford rumours abounded that the Rotherwas factory was to be closed, retained, expanded, or even would become the modern Woolwich, and these were reported in the local press during 1919. That year Winston Churchill, then War Minister, announced on 19 April that the Credenhill depot was to be used to disarm ammunition after which it would become a munitions store, whilst Rotherwas was to be retained. (Credenhill was to become an RAF camp during the Second World War and afterwards, and in 2000 it became the headquarters of the Special Air Service).

In April 1919, 923 people were still employed at Rotherwas.[10] The *Hereford Times* reported that there was considerable disquiet because people were holding on to jobs at the factory, rather than releasing them for demobed soldiers returning to the area. The paper published two letters in response to this concern. One read:

> The girls here are all local girls – girls who are compelled to earn their own living and who during the war worked their utmost to help and achieve victory. Why should we give up work which opened up for us during the war and has not robbed any man of his work.
>
> We are not all able to take domestic service and the work we have done and are doing is not suitable for some men. Girls have to live as well as discharged soldiers. So have over-age and rejected civilians, many of whom sent sons and brothers to fight for our country.[11]

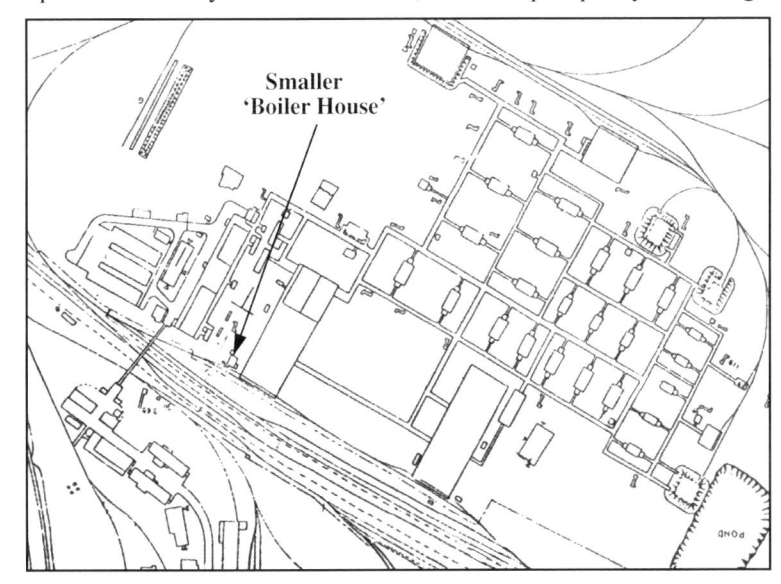

The Northern Section taken from a map dated 1942, showing significant changes from 1923 (opposite). A canteen and other buildings have ben erected to the west and several new buildings have been built on the central section

The other letter stated that many of those working at Rotherwas had originally been employed at the Banbury Filling Factory; Dilution only applied to firms that had released men and allowed women to take over their work.

In March 1920, the government confirmed that the filling factory at Hereford was to be retained on a permanent basis.[12] Even so, there was a need to rationalise and April 1920 saw the first of several auction sales at Rotherwas. This first sale included vegetable preserving equipment, a number of machine tools and a steam engine. Subsequent sales saw the disposal of two locomotives in December 1921 and the main railway platform and its footbridge in March 1923. It seems likely that some demolition of the covered corridors had taken place by 1923 as a large amount of Decauville 21 inch track was included in November's dispersal sale. Also auctioned was a standard gauge railway engine by Mannington Wardle and 1,000 steel sleepers for 24 inch track.[13]

On 13 April 1920 an explosion in the Northern Section occurred when two girls were counting fuzes, killing 20-year-old Winifred Aulsebrook and injuring Annie Tranter. By May the factory was employing 475 men and 245 women with a further 220 in the CSD stores.[14] The recovery of ammonium nitrate from its admixture with TNT to form amatol was said to have been undertaken at Hereford around 1920.[15]

In July a statement by C.F. Beakbane, the factory manager, that the breaking down of shrapnel shells was to be transferred to Woolwich, led to a statement in the House of Commons the following month confirming that Rotherwas was still earmarked for retention as part of the nucleus of ordnance factories. No part of the factory or the site would be sold off. Most of the remaining female staff had been given notice in July, but men continued to be employed in breaking down ammunition.[16]

The rumours of complete closure again surfaced in October and persisted into 1921. They were finally confirmed in March 1921 when the local M.P., Mr. S. Roberts, told the city council that most activities at Rotherwas were to cease, but it would remain in use as one of the principal War Office stores.[17] March

This building in the central section, identified as a hospital block by Dr. Mike Harrison, appears first on the 1923 plan where it is described as an oil and paint store. It is thought to be a 1920s addition, and is built of $4^{1}/_{2}$ inch brickwork with sprayed on concrete covering but without the piers found on other buildings constructed in 1916/17

also saw the demise of the Ministry of Munitions, with its remaining responsibilities being transferred to the War Office.[18]

On 5 March 1921 the *Hereford Times* reported that the factory was to close with all live ammunition being transferred to Woolwich. Of the 270 employed only 50 were retained including 13 policemen, 3 manning the boilers, 12 in the lyddite section and another 12 in engineering sections. At 10 p.m. on the day when most employees had been paid off there was a huge fire. A dump of empty ammunition boxes 200 x 50 yards and 30 feet high and an adjacent building burnt down. In November the *Hereford Times* reported that urgent work had begun to prevent the decay of ironwork at Rotherwas.

In the meantime, disarming of ammunition by George Cohen & Co. Ltd. had continued at Credenhill – not without incident. In January 1923 an explosion killed George Jones, a foreman, and severely injured a workman, Harold Lampitt. At the inquest it was disclosed that Jones was loosening black powder within a shell with a stick rather than washing it out because it was quicker. Jones died in the factory hospital.[19] In June there was another explosion, this time of an 18 pdr shell returned from France which killed one man. The shell was fitted with a type 100 fuze similar to that which had killed Winifred Aulsebrook in 1920 at Rotherwas. In evidence to the inquest Major McKenna, an Inspector of Safety Services in Breaking Down Ammunition said, in reply to the foreman of the Coroner's Jury, that the jolt of setting the shell down on a bench could be enough to make this fuze explode. The foreman who had served as a gunner in the war said the shells fitted with type 100 fuzes were regarded as very dangerous and were frequently 'prematures' exploding in the gun or earlier than wanted.

On a separate front, Hereford Rural District Council complained to George Cohen & Co. Ltd. that the burning of freed amatol from disarmed shells was injuring the health of the residents of Credenhill and turning cattle and sheep black. A number of letters on the subject were published in the *Hereford Times*. A Credenhill farmer was even brought before the magistrates accused of assaulting the factory manager over the matter, but the case was dismissed.[20]

1926 saw the demolition of Rotherwas House.[21]

In 1928 Rotherwas was proposed as the site for a new gunpowder factory but nothing came of the idea. The scheme was reconsidered in November 1930 but again rejected principally because of the possibility of flooding. Modernisation began in 1932 with the conversion of Unit 5 on the amatol section to enable it to fill naval mines, and later for depth charges and torpedoes. Other plant was added for further ammonium nitrate purification.[22]

After the General Election of 1935 rearmament began in earnest with the need to counter Germany's growing military strength, particularly that of the Luftwaffe. As expenditure on the armed forces grew, an increasing proportion went to the Royal Air Force. In 1935 the army received £40 million, the navy £56 million and the RAF £17 million. By 1939 the figures had soared, the navy receiving £127 million, the army £121 million and the RAF £133 million.[23]

The rearmament plans included the building of Royal Ordnance Factories at Chorley (Lancashire), Bridgend

(Glamorgan) and Glascoed (Monmouthshire), along with development at Hereford, though the precise nature of this depended upon whether Woolwich was run down or retained. With the decision to retain Woolwich at least until the new factories were fully operational, Hereford was notified at Christmas 1935 that it was to fill with amatol 1,000 to 2,000 250 lb bombs a month. Production began in October 1937 in Unit 5, with Unit 3 filling the same size of bomb with TNT as from January 1938. Equipment to fill the shells for the new 25 pdr gun and Unit 1, hot filling these munitions with TNT, was handed over on 16 August 1937. By October production was 6,000 shells a week. In August 1938 two more units – nos. 2 and 4 – for cold pressing amatol into 25 pdr shells were completed after being held up by changes to the design of filling equipment. Unit 6 had been filling torpedoes since 1933, and Unit 7 depth charges and torpedoes since October 1937. However, there is some confusion about what units 5 and 6 were filling. Unit 5 is described both as filling bombs and mines; Mrs. Peggy Jones who worked at the factory from mid 1940 stated that in 1941 she was filling 500lb bombs there.[24]

By September 1939 the Northern Section is thought to have been at work turning components into quick firing rounds. At 11.15 a.m. on Sunday 3 September, Great Britain went to war.

6   Chemical Warfare from 1918 onwards

The War Office took over responsibilities for supply of poison gases from the Ministry of Munitions on 1 July 1919 and by September 1919 all shells charged with gas had been 'cleared' – emptied or otherwise made harmless.[1] The widespread perception, too, is that with the ending of the war Britain ceased to have any gas warfare programme. However, Field Marshal Lord Carver suggests in *Britain's Army in the Twentieth Century* that there were two schools of thought at the end of the First World War. One thought that there should never again be such a war with its resulting carnage, the other that ways of waging war must be found which took less time and cost fewer lives. Within the proponents of the latter were air force strategists who favoured a decisive blow against the enemy's capital, probably using chemical bombs.[2] While the use of gas had had but limited success, it was still sufficient to imply that in the future it might have more – and to this end development of chemical warfare in fact continued.

Britain signed the Geneva Protocol in 1925 which prohibited the use of poisonous gases, chemical weapons and bacteriological methods of warfare and in 1930 changed the name of the experimental facilities at Porton Down (Dorset) from The Chemical Warfare Experimental Station to the Chemical Defence Experimental Station, Nevertheless, according to *Declaration re Chemical Warfare*, an official booklet held in the National Archives, Britain retained an offensive chemical warfare capability until 1959. It was thought necessary to continue with the development of new and better chemical agents in order to be able to defend the country against them – an argument still often used to justify certain expenditure. From this time all work on gas weapons was described as a study of chemical weapons against which defence was needed. Evidence exists to show that Rotherwas played a part in this when – as early as 1919 – staff from the filling factory at Banbury visited Hereford to see the production facilities for charging gas shells.[3] The equipment at Hereford, whilst based on that used at Banbury but installed later, would have been modified and improved in the light of Banbury's experience. Experiments into charging shells with mustard gas were carried out at Porton Down between 1924 and 1927, and correspondence from the War Office's Committee for Chemical Warfare Research was entered into with the Superintendent at Rotherwas, Digby Ovens, regarding suitable methods to avoid accidents, as casualties at Porton Down were considerable – with seven being incurred in charging just 2,000 shells.[4] The correspondence indicates that while the experiments were with head rather than side charging, the machines used were very similar to those installed at Hereford. This is an indication that the facilities at Hereford had by now been updated.

In an undated memo, the Committee for Chemical Warfare Research produced a list of necessary alterations to the equipment and changes in practice at Rotherwas. Their recommendations included the appointment of a doctor to oversee medical matters concerning gas charging, and Dr. William Ainslee was appointed

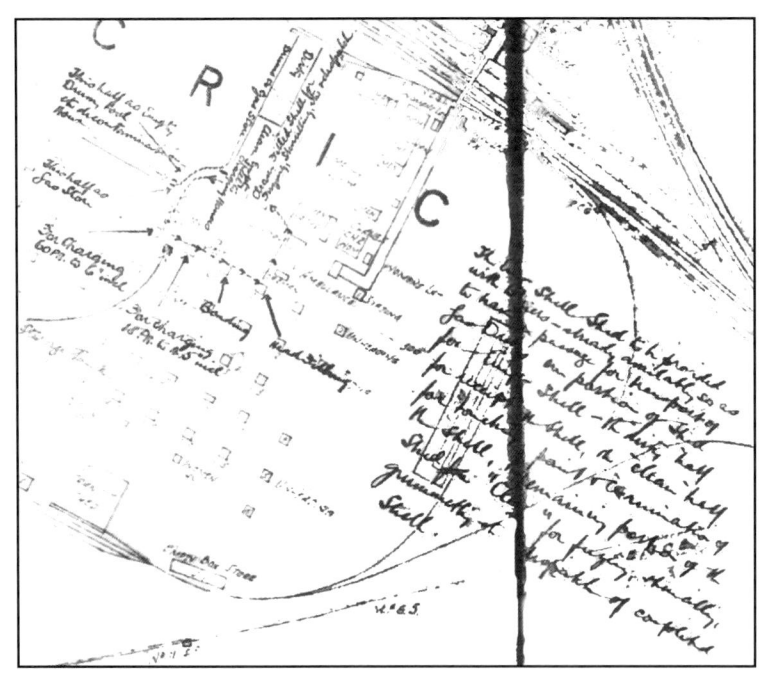

The 1926 copy of the map of 1919 marked up with the changes required to Unit 1 that would allow for shells to be charged with mustard gas. The note on the right reads: 'The empty shell store to be provided with barriers – already available, so as to make a passage for the transport of Gas Drums, a portion of the shed for empty shell – the 'dirty' half for receipt of shell, the 'clean' half for touching up paint and examination of the shell, the remaining portion of the shed for '?' for fusing, stencilling, grummetting etc., and dispatch of completed shell' (PRO SUPP 5/990)

on a part time basis – he was already responsible for the rest of the factory. He was directly charged with ensuring that he kept himself up-to-date with new developments regarding gas matters.[5] Dr. Ainslee had come to Hereford in 1912 to set up practice and had joined up in 1915, serving in the Medical Corps. He had won the MC before being invalided out of the army in 1918. He remained a leading figure in Hereford society and achieved national recognition for his work with X-Rays. He died in 1959 but is remembered in a photograph at the new Hereford County Hospital.[6]

In 1926 a copy of the 1919 map of the Northern Section was used by an unnamed colonel from CRE Welsh area (it is unclear what the initials stand for) to indicate the necessary changes to Unit 1 that would allow various sizes of shell to be charged with mustard gas. No archaeological evidence that these specific proposals were carried out has been found. However, a two page document, dated 24 February 1927, and entitled *Gas Shell*, is signed by Digby Ovens and reads as if the activities described were taking place at Rotherwas – at a time when officially Rotherwas was no more than a storage depot. The paper details the process of charging with gas and filling with explosive and mentions that there are variations with 'large calibre shell such as 6 inch etc.'. Charging, it states, was now done by the C.I.A. (Civilian Inspectorate of Ammunition) who were also responsible for weighing and final examination.[7]

The D. of A. (presumably the Department of Armaments) produced a document dated 28 March 1927 and sent it to the Committee for Chemical Warfare Research stating that Hereford was equipped to charge (with gas) and head fill (with explosive) the following weekly outputs of shells, once the order had been given:

	End of 4th week	End of 8th week	End of 12th week
18 pdr	Nil	30,000 or	60,000 or
3.7 inch	Nil	18,000 or	36,000 or
4.5 inch	Nil	12,500	25,000

This implies that the numbers of machines for charging had been increased since November 1918 when only around 4,000 shells had been charged in a four week period.

There were, they added, machines in store for charging 6 and 9.2 inch shells and that Rotherwas was the only factory equipped to charge large quantities of shells with gas.[8] The Committee for Chemical Warfare Research responded in a memo dated 2 April, proposing that Porton should be responsible for charging all gas weapons, whilst Sutton Oak (St. Helen's, Lancashire) should develop the necessary manufacturing processes. In addition, the experimental facilities for producing mustard gas at Sutton Oak should be expanded to allow for the production of 20 tons a week. The memo noted that Hereford had been retained with much of its wartime charging equipment intact.

A meeting at the War Office on 18 May 1927 considered Hereford's future and decided that it might be necessary to erect mustard gas production units at the factory, but that the question of installing any manufacturing plant would await discussion on war requirements.

For the Department of Finance at the War Office, G.S. Whitham wrote to the C.S.O.F. – thought to stand for Chief Scientific Officer – at Woolwich on 13 January 1928, mentioning a new gas charging plant at Hereford.[9] On 26 January he wrote to a Mr. Hinles saying that it had been accepted that the head filling (with a high explosive burster charge) of chemical shells should be carried out at Hereford.[10]

Members of the Committee for Chemical Warfare Research visited Hereford on 26 February to ascertain the condition of the charging equipment and they concluded that it would be of great value if the 50 men employed there could be relied upon to train new employees in charging gas shells if war were to come.[11] This is the last direct mention of gas charging at Hereford. The following year expenditure on chemical warfare preparations amounted to £156,823 – the Chemical Warfare Department cost £24,231, Porton Down £114,712 and Sutton Oak £17,880. No expenditure on Hereford is recorded, but a large building scheme likely to cost £118,000 was 'threatened', although the document does not state where.[12]

Through the early part of the 1930s the Treasury tried hard to cap expenditure on chemical warfare, but on 7 July 1936 gave permission to erect a plant to manufacture HS mustard gas jointly with ICI with a capacity to produce 50 tons a week.[13] This was the plant at Randle (Merseyside) which came into production in 1938.[14]

This leaves a gap between 1927/9 and 1936 where no documentary evidence has been found concerning the country's development of an offensive chemical warfare capability. Yet the 1959

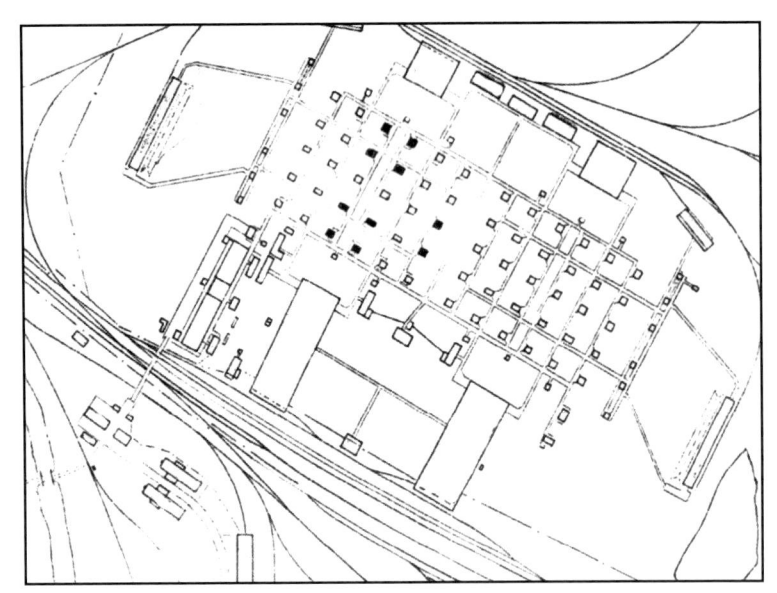

The Northern Section as shown on a map of 1923. The buildings filled in in black are known to have been used for work with mustard gas when Unit 1 was charging shells at the end of the war. The 'boiler house' to the west of the western empty shell store appears on a map for the first time – see detail to the right. This detail shows a number of new buildings that appear on a map for the first time, including an oil and paint store, identified by Dr. Mike Harrison, a retired Medical Officer of Health, as a hospital (see also page 50). At some time, probably during the 1930s modernisation a large gas decontamination unit was added. While Cocroft in Dangerous Energy *states that such decontamination units were usual at ROFs this was a very large unit indeed (see photograph opposite)*

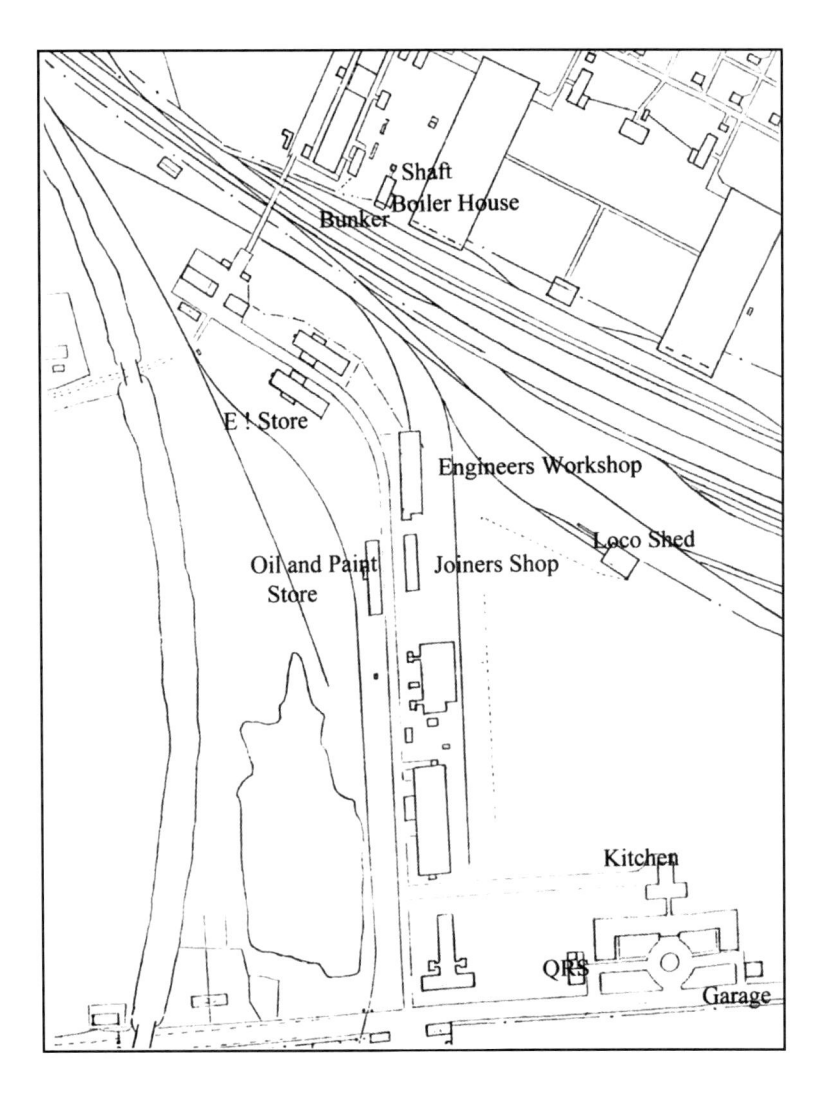

Declaration re Chemical Warfare states that as international tension developed in the 1930s steps were indeed taken to develop that offensive capability.

The references to Hereford over these years essentially relate to the factory's capacity to charge gas shells yet include little evidence that any form of chemical warfare product was directly handled. However, in addition to the documents quoted there is archaeological evidence.

Immediately to the west of the empty shell store of Unit 1 of the Northern Section is a building which is described on a map of 1942 as a boiler house. It first appears as a larger building on the 1924 map. The Northern Section during both wars was a secure area where explosives were handled and workers entering were subject to strict controls about bringing in anything likely to cause an explosion. It seems most unlikely that a coal-fired boiler house would be erected inside such an area. A study of the plans of other First and Second World War filling factories shows their boiler houses well isolated from secure areas.

The quality of the construction of the building marked as a 'boiler house' on the 1924 map is considerably better than that of the known First World War buildings on the site, suggesting it

The decontamination building of circa *1938, a large building compared to those at other ordnance factories and some ten shower stalls have been identified inside. The lean-to on the left housed a heater*

The east and north walls of the 'boiler house'. The lean-to on the left is thought to have housed a large air compressor. The outside of the north wall, to the right, is an infill and there is thought to have been an original fifth bay nearer the camera (Andrew Terry, Herefordshire Council)

was built after the end of the war. The building has subsequently been modified on a number of occasions, some of which look to have been done hurriedly. There is no evidence to confirm that this building was in fact a boiler house: there is a total lack of smoke staining to the walls or roof, and despite the map showing what looks to be factory-type chimney stack, there is no sign of any connection between the stack and the boiler house. The stack has totally disappeared. Between the 'boiler house' and the empty shell store a small complex of raised, narrow, concrete pathways survive. No logical explanation of what use these were put to has been found.

The mystery surrounding Unit 1 deepens when the factory was redeveloped in the late 1930s to turn Rotherwas into a more versatile filling factory. This investment provided it with the ability to fill a far wider range of munitions than had been handled during the First World War, including both breech loading munitions and quick firing ammunition. By 1937 all of the buildings on the Northern Section other than the picric acid stores, the two empty shell stores and the two transit sheds had been demolished and the wooden corridors removed.[15] Work then began on the construction of the wooden buildings – 16 large, eight medium sized and one very small – which were used during the Second World War. Each was surrounded by concrete blast walls. These buildings filled cartridges with cordite and then connected these with shells filled with explosive on the Southern Section to form quick firing ammunition. All but one of the wooden sheds and two other buildings are sited on what was Unit 2 of the Northern Section in the First World War – yet almost all of the area occupied by Unit 1 was cleared and left undeveloped. A 1941 aerial photograph shows this (see the grassy humps in the top left of the photograph on page 66) and provides evidence that in common with other open areas within the factory the ground was either kept free of vegetation or was mown. No explanation has been found as to why most of the area of Unit 1 remained undeveloped.

The documents found in the National Archives together with the archaeological evidence do not, unfortunately, provide proof that either the manufacture of mustard gas or the charging of shells with the gas went on at Rotherwas in the inter-war years. What they do show is that a great deal of thought and effort was put into the possibility of such developments, in which Rotherwas played an important part.

7 Rotherwas at War – 1939 to 1945

With the rearmament programme which had begun in earnest in the middle of the decade together with the shadow factory building programme inaugurated in the summer of 1936, industrially the country was somewhat more prepared than in 1914. Shadow factories were built by the bigger industrial firms using government capital on the understanding that in the event of war they would be available for munitions production. Many of the factories were situated well away from the traditional industrial areas in an attempt to limit damage from air attacks, but because of the area's engineering skills six were built in the Coventry area. Shadow factories were employing almost 25,000 people by 1943 and were responsible for much of the aircraft production throughout the war. The Castle Bromwich (Warwickshire) shadow factory planned and built by Nuffield but run by Vickers, was vitally important at the time of the Battle of Britain when it kept up its production of Spitfires at a time of heavy losses. Locally, Spitfire radiators were manufactured at Lanfoist near to Abergavenny, and at Newtown (Powys) gun turrets for Barracuda aircraft were made. But in many ways Britain was slow to organise itself, seemingly almost preferring not to accept the reality of war. Secretary of State for War, Sir Kingsley Wood said in 1939 in reply to a Parliamentary question suggesting that German forests should be set on fire: 'Are you not aware that they are private property? You will be asking me to bomb Essen next'.[1]

The planned expansion of Royal Ordnance Factories was under way but far from complete. By December 1939 they were employing 54,200 people (9,900 employed in filling) of whom nearly half were at Woolwich.[2] In the next 12 months the number was to double to 112,900 (49,300 in filling) and to peak in June 1942 at 302,100.[3] The greatest number employed in filling munitions was in March 1942 when the numbers reached 153,100. During 1941 the Ministry of Supply, responsible for providing labour for the Royal Ordnance factories and a large number of private contractors, was taking on 9,500 workers each week.

Attempting to avoid a similar situation to that which occurred during the early part of the First World War when skilled workers volunteering for the army dramatically reduced output at many vital factories, in September 1939 the government introduced the Control of Employment Act to limit the movement of skilled men. Under this Act an employer could register those regarded as essential who were then exempt from call-up and were prevented from leaving their job. Then in May 1940 industrial conscription for men was brought in and was extended to women in December 1941, meaning that both men and women could be directed to a particular job.[4]

The loss of equipment in the evacuation from Dunkirk in 1940 meant that there was a desperate shortage of all forms of munitions, and for a time the Royal Ordnance Factories operated a 70 to 75 hour working week, based around two, eleven hour shifts, seven days a week. In the first week output was up by 25% but it was quickly apparent that sheer fatigue actually reduced outputs. Sunday working was abandoned and a three shift, eight hour, six

Hand stemming a 9.2 inch shell at Hereford during the First World War, a system still is use in the Second World War since it was found to be faster than an interwar mechanized compaction process, and according to anecdotal evidence it became the standard process employed at Rotherwas (IWM Q70679)

day week system, with limited overtime, introduced.[5] By 1941 the regular working week had been stabilised at 55 to 56 hours.

Productivity in the Royal Ordnance Factories rose dramatically during the war. They were among the first UK firms to introduce three-shift working, and they were far ahead of private industry in their use of time and motion studies, the application of incentives, and statistical methods of quality control.[6] Many of the problems that had arisen during the First World War were addressed – crèches were established; canteens were built; a travelling allowance of 10s. a day to cover the costs of the journey to work was paid, and an allowance of 24s. 6d. was available to cover the first week's lodgings before wages had been earned.[7] In terms of the conscription of women, Britain went further than any other combatant – including Russia and Germany. The proportion of women in the forces, munitions and other essential industries was twice that of the First World War.[8]

By the autumn of 1943 the Allied output of all forms of war material had far outstripped that of the Axis powers. Production was no longer a problem and manpower began to be transferred from industry to the armed forces.[9] But there was a catch. Production figures had almost become an end in themselves. An assistant to Professor Jukes of Manchester University wrote:

> The veneration paid to figures increased when they were neatly presented in well laid out tables and reached its height if the tables were printed. The worship of statistics helped to produce a frame of mind in which the production of useless aircraft was preferred to the production of no aircraft at all.

Vast stocks of artillery ammunition had been accumulated because production targets were based on usage during the First World War, and by the end of 1942 this had resulted in endless roadside dumps of shells, many of which were not cleared until well after the end of the war.[10]

A shell, likely to have been filled at Rotherwas, exploded in one such roadside dump at Wigmore, north Herefordshire, in 1946 and a gang of youths were brought before the magistrates accused of stealing a large number of exploders. In evidence an army officer said that there had been interference with some 500 shells. He suggested that within an area of 300 square miles there were 10,000 shell dumps, with notices simply warning of the danger. They were only visited on an occasional basis, perhaps no more often than once every two weeks.[11]

The war saw immense technological changes in weapons. John Terraine writing in *The Right of the Line* states that in 1939 British bombs were as awful as had been the mines and torpedoes produced in the First World War. He continues:

> For a variety of reasons which included the procreative habits of cockles and the peace of mind of swans the provision of ranges for the proper testing of bombs proved impossible in peace time and difficult even in wartime.

The first attack on a submarine was made by an Anson of RAF Coastal Command in the middle of September 1939. The aircraft dropped two 100lb bombs which bounced off the water and exploded under the aircraft. This ruptured the petrol tanks and the aircraft had to make a forced landing on the sea. The submarine belonged to the British navy! In another practice attack the aircraft managed to drop a 100lb bomb on the conning tower of a submarine – causing sufficient damage to require the changing of four light bulbs.

RDX, a much more powerful explosive than amatol, was introduced in 1940 and production facilities were installed in the Royal Ordnance Factory at Bridgwater (Somerset), but as late as 1944 much of this explosive still came from America. In 1939 the Blenheim twin-engined bomber with a crew of three carried a payload of two 500lb bombs for no great distance. By 1945 specially modified Lancasters crewed by seven airmen were capable of delivering Grand Slams weighing in at a massive 21,000lb anywhere in Germany. Anti-tank ammunition began the war as 2lb solid rounds and developed into hollow nosed ammunition capable of penetrating ever thicker armour plate. As a result the Royal Ordnance factories were constantly altering their production methods, the changes usually increasing the hazards inherent in filling work, with some rounds of ammunition containing as many as 40 different components.[12]

Being well away from London, and with the likelihood of aerial attacks thought to be low, a large number of buildings across Herefordshire, including all the city centre hotels, were requisitioned by various government departments at the outbreak of war.[13] Accommodation in and around Hereford, whether it was in lodgings, housing or military barracks, was in short supply even before the outbreak of the war. Hereford's population at 30,000 in 1939 was rapidly increasing. They were soon joined by the first intake of 1,500 recruits at the newly built Bradbury Lines on 16 July.[14] On 9 September the *Hereford Times* reported the arrival of 850 evacuees. In December the council was told that the city had to find accommodation for another 6,000 people and that the population was likely to reach 40,000.[15] Staff were being moved to Rotherwas from Woolwich, felt to be vulnerable to bombing raids due to being easily visible alongside a river feeding into the Thames Estuary, and the numbers there were planned to drop to around 5,000.[16] Those who moved soon discovered that they were paid £2 10s. a week less than they had been paid in London.[17]

At the outbreak of the war Rotherwas was employing 1,000 people, a similar number to those then filling munitions at the new but far from complete Royal Ordnance Factory at Chorley.[18] The factory was controlled by a superintendent, equivalent to a factory general manager, but he did not have full authority over welfare, canteens, housing and some aspects of labour matters. The administration needed by the soon to be rapidly expanded workforce was to pose considerable problems for management.[19] To increase the numbers and quality of welfare officers at ordnance factories, their wages were increased by 50% in 1940.[20]

By July 1940 Rotherwas was employing 4,600 people – 2,500 on the Southern Filling Factory and 2,100 on the Northern Assembly Section.[21] In a repeat of First World War events, the first offenders to be brought before the magistrates for taking matches into the factory were fined and warned that in future others would face prison.[22]

The Deputy Divisional Controller of the Ministry of Labour for the Midlands had addressed a meeting at Hereford in June at which he said that 1,400 women aged between 18 and 50 were immediately required at Rotherwas. Those over 21 were told they would earn a basic minimum wage of £1 12s. a week for a 47 hour week, but that average earnings for 55 hours was £2 7s. 6d. or £3 5s. for a 60 hour week. If necessary, those evacuees billeted in the city would be moved away to provide accommodation for Rotherwas workers. Employees were to be taken on by the Labour Exchange and transport was to be provided to the factory either by bus or train.[23] Later in the month the Mayor established a crèche. With the overall increase in population in the district considerable strain was put on the waterworks, and an extension to the sand beds to be paid for by the Ministry of Supply was approved. Despite all these efforts there was a shortage of workers at Hereford in the winter of 1940/41.[24]

In November 1939 the Hereford Deanery Committee were concerned that evacuees were failing to attend Sunday School. In July 1940 they reported to the Bishop their unease that young girls were hanging about the streets and 'attaching' themselves to soldiers. The Bishop took no action. The Committee suggested to the factory superintendent that they would be happy to organise regular 15 minute services on a Sunday at Rotherwas. He did not reply until September 1940 when he told them that Sunday working had stopped. In October they asked the Home Guard to alter the times of their Sunday parades to allow members to attend church. In December, they tried, and failed, to appoint a chaplain at the factory as had been done during the First World War.[25]

In the meantime the Ministry of Health wrote to the Town Clerk suggesting that the Women's Voluntary Organisation (later the Women's Royal Voluntary Service) should help in obtaining billets for the girls coming to Rotherwas, and that an appeal should be made to find more lodgings. A census in August found that 700 lodging places were available and that this might be extended to 1,000. A Reception Committee with members drawn from the council and the factory was formed. At a September meeting in London, the Town Clerk stressed that Hereford was at bursting point and was assured that unless there was a military emergency no further troops would be billeted in the city. In October, the Ministry of Health extended Regulation 22 of the Defence Regulations making billeting compulsory and a Mr. Hulbard was appointed Chief Billeting Assistant at an annual salary of £300. He was called up on 5 December and Mr. Weston was appointed in his place. Some households were duly officially notified that they would be required to take lodgers, charges for lodgings being set at 5s. a week; November saw the first fines for those refusing to take in lodgers.[26] Proposals to build a hostel surfaced in August and are covered in the next chapter.

On 3 July 1940 the first bombs to be dropped on the county exploded at Much Marcle but there was little damage and no casualties.[27]

In September the *Hereford Times* reported a serious explosion that killed three people and injured three others at a 'West Country Royal Ordnance Factory'. The paper was banned under censorship laws from being overly specific, and the phrase became its euphemism for the Rotherwas factory. At the inquest held in October, questions were asked about the safety record of the incorporation mill in which the explosion had occurred and doubts were expressed about the way in which a bearing had been replaced.[28] Unconfirmed oral evidence from Mrs. Peggy Jones, then working on the Southern Section, suggests that the explosion was caused by one of those killed who was working in the incorporation house. Notified that the Dangerous Buildings Officer – who was responsible for safety matters and who had the power to search people – was approaching, he threw some snuff he had into the mill and it was this impurity which caused the explosion.[29]

Workers were drawn from a wide area. Those fined in the magistrates court for carrying contraband over a three week period lived in Hereford, Leominster, Ross-on-Wye as well as Little Birch, Llangrove and Peterchurch in Herefordshire, along with Cinderford, Malvern, Monmouth, and Retford (Nottinghamshire).

In the middle of 1940 the empty shell store of Unit 1 on the Northern Section was preparing 3.7 inch anti-aircraft shells for filling. After cleaning, the shells were first internally painted with shellac and then externally before the shells were fed through an oven to dry. They were then taken to the Southern Section for filling and thence came back to the new buildings on the Northern Section to be joined to a cordite-filled, brass cartridge case.[30] Later, with the development of anti-aircraft rocket batteries, production shifted to 25 pdr, the most commonly used shell of the Second World War.

1941 was to see the invasion of Russia which took the pressure off this country, the Luftwaffe largely ending the Blitz, and the

Japanese attack on Pearl Harbour that brought the United States into the war.

Locally Rotherwas became an established filling factory, training recruits who were then sent on to the new factories.[31] Conscription for women between 19 and 40 was brought in in March and by August two million had registered but only 87,000 had been called up.[32] The Essential Works Order of March 1941 introduced labour direction – enabling the government to direct factories to produce specific products as well as giving the Ministry of Labour draconian powers over workpeople – but its powers were in fact gently applied with the aim of avoiding the labour problems of the First World War.[33]

The Ministry of Health informed the city council of the difficulty of transferring essential workers (from Woolwich) because they were unable to find accommodation for wives and family, and that the ministry was taking powers to bring in the Billeting Act in this area, which made it compulsory to take in lodgers where there was spare accommodation, but the council decided to object. In November Mr. Weston resigned and his deputy, G.W. Parsons, was appointed at a reduced salary of £250. In December the Ministry of Health wrote to the council asking for the number

Right: This carefully posed picture shows what was the standard anti-aircraft gun at the beginning of the war, the 3.7 inch, mobile AA gun. The Northern Section at Rotherwas, fully operational at the outbreak of war, was occupied in assembling the filled shell and the cartridge to produce a complete quick firing round as held by the soldier in the foreground.
(Birmingham at War Volume 1)

employed in the billeting department to be raised from four to five.[34]

During the early part of 1941 the Dean, his committee and the members of Hereford District Council met with the Factory Superintendent, Digby Ovens, and the Factory Welfare Officer, Mrs. H.E. Wit. The latter was scathing in her criticism of the treatment many of the girls were receiving from their landladies, with many being excluded from their accommodation at weekends. It was agreed that the clergy would in future be provided with details of new arrivals so that they might monitor the situation. In March the committee was regretting the opening of the theatre on a Sunday. In May the committee received a letter from the deputy manager for the Holiday Fellowship who were to run the new Red Hill Hostel, stating that it would soon be handed over and that there was to be a devotional house with regular Sunday services. It was agreed to hold services at the new hostel but the hours suggested did not fit in with the wants of the committee. Correspondence on this matter was to go on for more than 12 months. In June the Dean told his committee that for several weeks he had promised to be 'at home' at the factory between 8 and 9 p.m. on Wednesday evenings for any factory worker who might want to see him, but 'that no one ever came'.[35]

In September another explosion occurred at Rotherwas, again in an incorporating mill, in which three people were killed and six injured. At the inquest held in October there were reports that this particular mill had previously overheated, although the explosion was caused by one of the rollers coming off its spindle. The following February the *Hereford Times* reported that the British Empire Medal had been awarded to two workers who had rescued those injured, noting that the building had been badly damaged and was in imminent danger of collapse when the two men saved others trapped on the second floor.[36]

Early 1942 was perhaps the darkest period of the war with the loss of many of Britain's far-east colonies and German successes in the Battle of the Atlantic. The basic petrol ration was abolished,

*The more effective rocket projector in July 1942. This weapon fired rockets whose explosive charge was filled, according to Mrs. Carmichael, in Unit 2 of the south section at Rotherwas. The picture shows the Home Guard manning the rocket projectors (*Birmingham at War *Volume 2)*

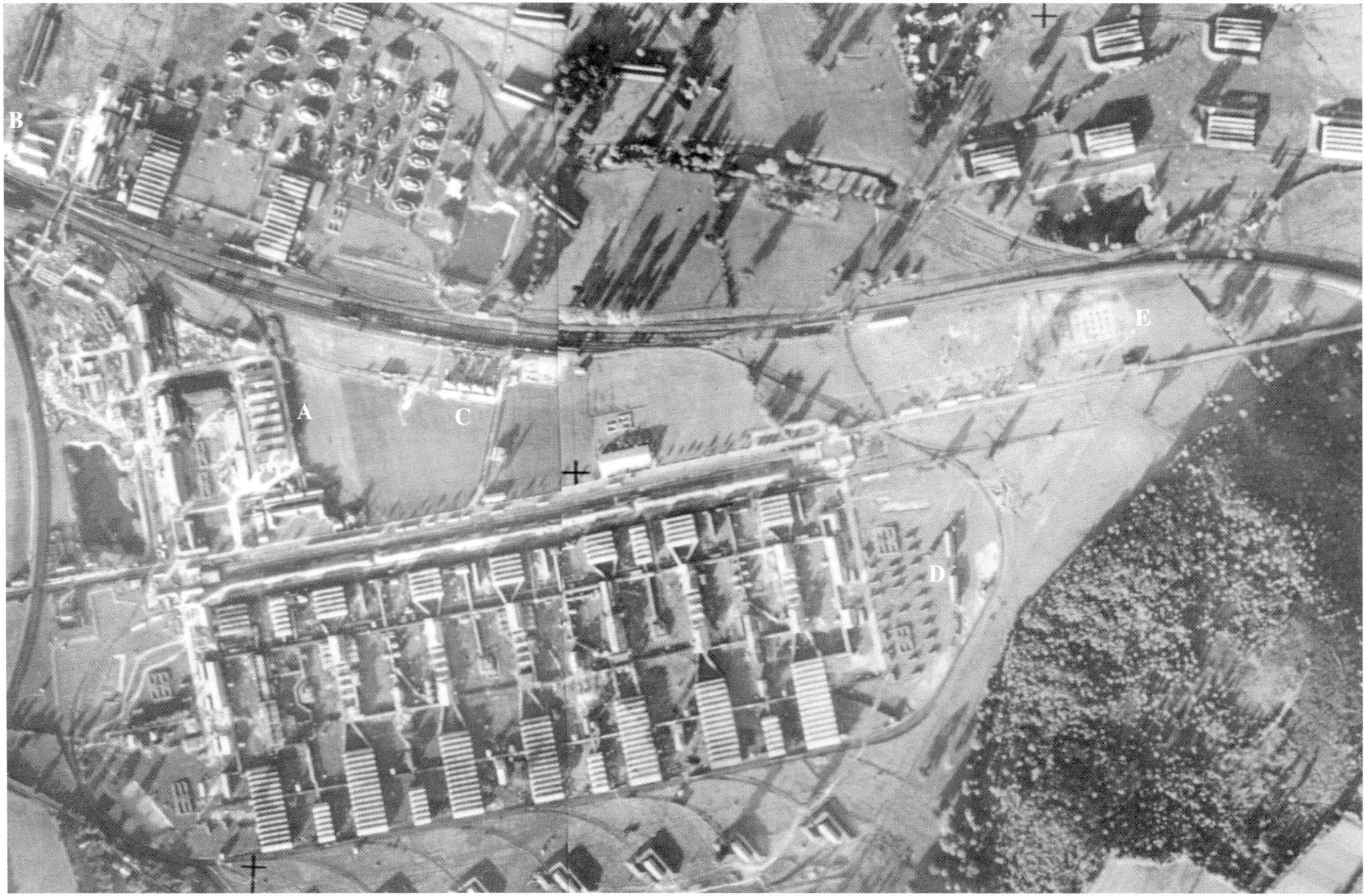
B
A
C
E
D

ending all private motoring and most cars were stored for the duration of the war, raised on bricks to save their tyres.[37] In February Air Marshall Sir Arthur Harris was appointed commander of Bomber Command and while he ended the year with around the same number of operational aircraft as at the beginning, they were new types of aircraft that could carry a greater payload of larger individual bombs producing an increase in demand from the filling factories.[38] This process had started the previous year, when the first 4,000lb 'blockbuster' bomb was delivered on 30 March and used for the first time in North Africa.[39] Also in 1942, towards the end of the year, American servicemen began to arrive in the UK as part of Operation Bolero, which led locally to the building of the camp at Moreton-on-Lugg.[40]

The minimum wage at Rotherwas for a week without overtime was now £3 but better rates of pay could be obtained in other jobs, although those handling explosives did receive additional danger

Left: An RAF aerial photograph taken on 22 October 1941. A number of buildings have been added in the Central Section including the large Civilian Inspectorate of Ammunition shed (A). Reconstruction of the Northern Section is complete and the canteen (B) to the west has been added. Fireman's Row (C) is just to the south of the lake formed when aggregate for the building work was dug. A large block of 'Z' type air raid shelters (D) with two of the larger above ground types are shown to the east of Unit 7 of the Southern Section. The foundations for the first of what was to become four new storage buildings have been dug (E)
(NMR Film No. 13N/UK 795 Frame 139 and 142)

money. Two girls who left without the permission of the National Service Officer at Rotherwas were fined £5 each and ordered to return.[41]

The event of 1942 most vividly remembered by those working at Rotherwas was the bombing. Early in the morning of 27 July a lone German bomber circled the site and dropped its bomb load, thought to be of 250kg high explosive bombs.

Mr. Evans, Deputy Head-warden of the St. Martin's ARP group from 1938 to 1946 is quoted in a very detailed document as saying that the raid occurred at 6 a.m., but it seems likely to have been somewhat later. Mr. Evans stated that an elderly lady to whom he talked (the way it is written suggests that this was possibly in 1991, the date of the document) and who worked at the factory was told at the time that all the casualties occurred in the road outside the factory area,[42] a view confirmed by two other witnesses, which would indicate the bombs hit when workers were arriving at 6.30 a.m., ready to start the new shift half an hour later.[43]

With no official account of the bombing raid, several differing versions of what occurred have been found. What is without doubt is that once the bomber had found the factory it circled before making a run across the site from the south-east in a curve towards the south-west. Mrs. Taylor was cycling into work from between Holme Lacy and Fownhope where her parents were landlords of the local pub. The bomber passed over her heading west, low enough for her to suggest that had she had a broomstick she could have poked it. It then peeled away to the south and flew over the factory dropping its bombs.[44] Another eyewitness stated that the bomber flew so low that she could see the pilot grinning as he dropped his bombs.[45]

It would seem that the first bomb landed on the Holme Lacy road where buses were delivering the new shift and waiting to collect those finishing their night shift. It was here that most of the casualties were incurred, with 17 people killed and 24 injured. One of those killed was uncle to a Mr. G. Morris. The family lived in Leominster and both his mother and her brother worked at Rotherwas.[46] Mrs. Margaret Smith's mother and father were both working at Rotherwas at the time of the explosion. Her mother was killed and her father was awarded a medal for bravery after the raid. She stated that people getting off the buses waved at the plane thinking it was British.[47] This was confirmed orally by another elderly person who worked at Rotherwas at the time.[48]

A second bomb hit the transit shed of Unit 2 in the Southern Section destroying it. It is not clear if any filled munitions were in the store at the time or if any casualties were incurred here. Map evidence and aerial photographs confirm that this shed had been destroyed.

Ken Hursey's recollection of the behaviour of the third bomb is recorded in Mr. Evans' account of the raid. Then aged 15, Ken was the youngest son of Police Superintendent E.J. Hursey who was in charge of the factory police. They lived at Moorlands Villa, just outside the western perimeter of the factory. Sleeping in the house that morning were Superintendent and Mrs. Hursey, their son Corporal P. Hursey, home on leave from the RAF, their daughter-in-law Mrs. V. Hursey and her mother.

Because of the presence of Mrs. V. Hursey and her mother, Ken was sleeping in a temporary bedroom in the disused granary next door. He heard the bomber and looked out of the window to see it drop two bombs onto the transit shed. One exploded and the other was deflected by a girder and came skidding along the ground passing through the wire fence to enter his parents' house where it exploded. The next thing he knew was someone shouting 'Is anyone alive?' This was Mr. Evans, and Ken was subsequently dug out totally uninjured by the Hereford ARP Rescue Team from under 14ft of rubble. But the five members of his family were killed. The site of Moorlands Villa is now rough ground.[49]

A study of the aerial photographs and maps suggests the story cannot be completely true.[50] The distance between the transit shed and Moorlands Villa is approximately 400 yards and at least two sets of buildings are in the way (see the plan opposite). However, Mr. Evans does state that he received a message from the Royal Ordnance Factory ARP saying that an unexploded bomb had been 'noticed' passing through the transit shed towards Moorlands Villa. Two houses close to Moorlands Villa were only slightly damaged. Their occupants had sheltered in the air raid shelters and were unhurt.

There is also some confusion about a possible fourth bomb. Mrs. Peggy Jones, a checker in Unit 6 of the Southern Section where she was in charge of three others filling 250lb bombs was in a toilet washing off her protective make-up supplied by Max Factor before going home. She heard the sound of a bomber and thought it to be German – twin-engined German aircraft could be distinguished by the sound of their unsynchronised engines. She stood on a toilet seat to see out of the window, but the next thing she recalled was finding herself sitting on the floor with her back against the wall and staring at the nose of a German bomb resting

Transit Shed

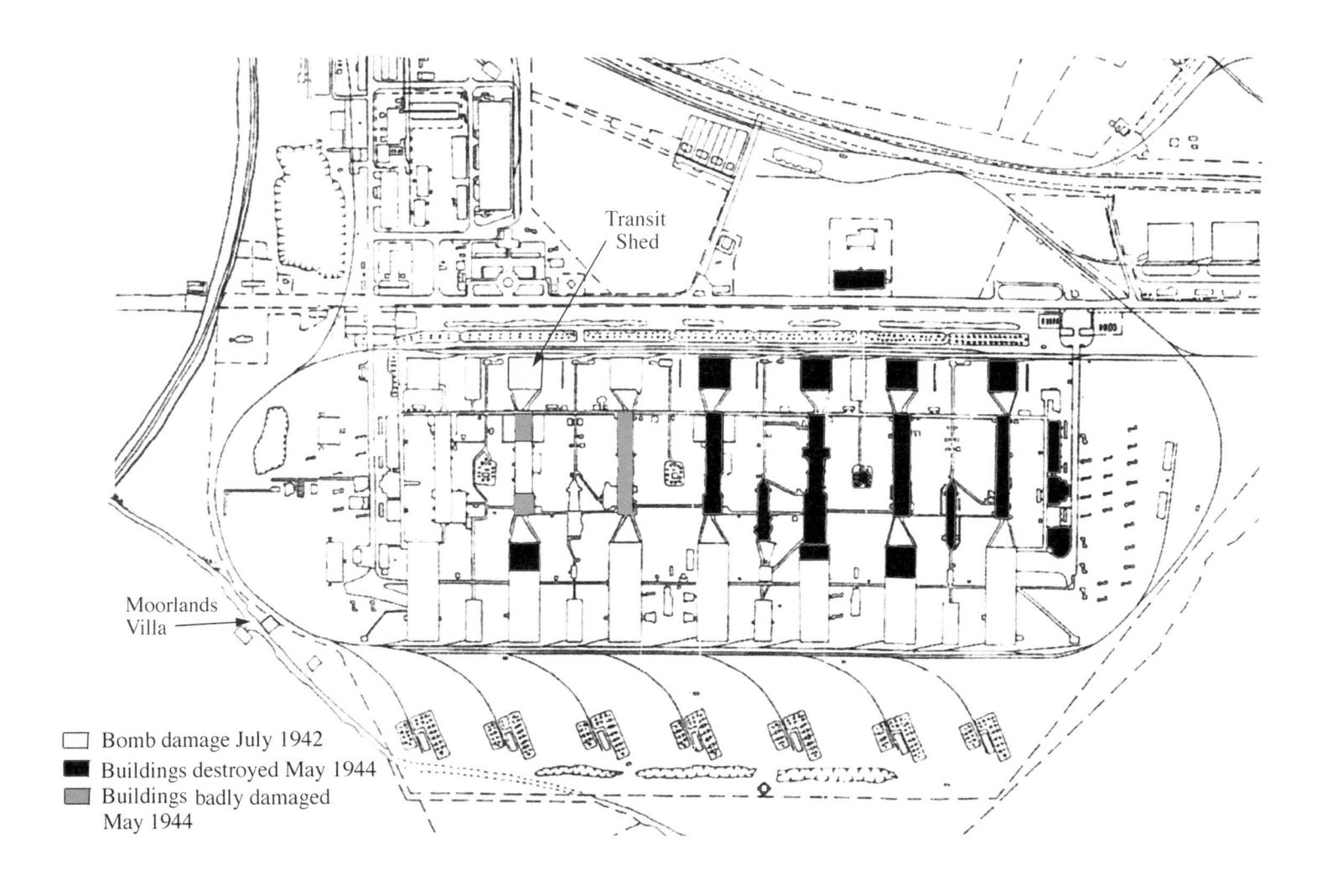

Moorlands Villa

☐ Bomb damage July 1942
■ Buildings destroyed May 1944
▨ Buildings badly damaged May 1944

69

part way through the opposite wall. She said she was absolutely certain at this point that the bomb would not go off and when examined by the bomb disposal squad stationed on the site – she referred to them as the suicide squad – the detonator was found to missing. Confirmation of this story is lacking.[51] Another account by Mrs. Doris Evans of Little Dewchurch suggests that an unexploded bomb passed through a shed in Unit 3.

The bombing also cut some electrical power to the Southern Section. Mrs. Gittings was alone, filling 25pdr shells in a small press house. When the bombs went off the light went out leaving her in total darkness. The door locks automatically came in making it impossible for her to leave the building. The fact that it took ten hours to release her is perhaps a major reason why she so vividly recalled the incident.[52]

The ARP remained on site until 4 p.m. working to ensure that no human remains were left in the area. So many people came to look at the damage that a section of troops was sent to control the crowd.[53] Another eyewitness related that for months following the raid a woman's nightdress hung from a tree in the garden of Moorlands Villa.[54]

There was a heavy machine gun post in the central area close to Fireman's Row but at the time of the bombing the crew had been stood down because there was little enemy air activity. Other accounts state that the ammunition for the gun was locked up and the key could not be found or that the gun was dismantled. Local anecdotal evidence says that the plane was pursued by Spitfires from Madley RAF aerodrome a few miles from Hereford and eventually shot down over the Bristol Channel.[55]

In October 1942 a third accidental explosion occurred at Rotherwas, this time in a shell filling house, killing two men and injuring four women. At the inquest it was reported that the two men had been loading filled and fuzed shells on to a trolley when one exploded. It was concluded that the fuze had probably been wrongly assembled and the jar of setting the shell down on the trolley had set it off.[56] In December one of 12 railway wagons making up an ammunition train from the factory blew up near Leominster. There were no casualties.[57]

During the year the Dean's committee remained concerned at the level of pastoral care and requested the Bishop to appoint a full time chaplain to the Red Hill Hostel. In May they had found that the Methodists had already appointed a woman evangelist, and they appealed to the Board of District Finance to meet the cost of a chaplain and if that failed, to approach the State with a view to them 'shouldering the burden'. The Vicar of St. Martin's introduced a note of common sense when he suggested there was no need for services at the hostel as his church was no more than 100 yards away. But still the committee wanted to appoint a Church Army captain and decided to offer anyone willing to serve, a stipend of £150 per annum.[58]

The hostels were usually only half full, most preferring the more home-like atmosphere of lodging with a family. But for some girls the hostels offered an escape from slum conditions, often providing them with a room of their own for the first time ever – and a bath with running water.[59]

During the year the senior regional officer of the Ministry of Health and his assistant met members of the council as they wanted to impose a Lodging Restriction Order in Hereford. This would have brought in severe rules covering the numbers of people boarded in any one household. The council replied that there was no need unless there was a big influx of workers.[60]

The Control of Engagement Order brought in on 16 February 1942 made it compulsory for all employers to only take on women through their local employment exchange. In the autumn conscription of women was extended to those aged up to 45,[61] and the local newspapers published details each week of those who had to register.[62]

Pontrilas Ordnance Storage Depot opened sometime during 1942 and was used to store explosives for use at Rotherwas.[63] It consisted of two locomotive sheds and 19, well spaced, above ground, storage buildings each served by a railway branch.[64] It remains in military ownership. A second storage depot for filled munitions was situated at Haywood and was served by a link to the main line. Thought to have been opened in 1942 it was returned to private ownership in the 1950s.

Aerial photographic evidence shows that there was an extensive building programme at Rotherwas during 1942 – a new boiler house was under construction in the Central Section and the foundation work for the first of four large storage buildings on the Eastern Section was underway.[65]

The following year saw the war shift strongly in favour of the Allies. In the Battle of the Atlantic the introduction of the Hedgehog depth charge launchers and the later heavier version, the Squid, which threw depth charges ahead of the ship firing them, helped to turn the tide.[66] As the bombing campaign grew in intensity the filling factories placed greater emphasis on bomb filling.[67] Questions can be asked as to the effectiveness of the bombing of Germany but it did lessen Germany's strength in Russia. The invading German army in 1942 was supported by more than half the Luftwaffe. By the end of 1943 this proportion was down to less than one fifth as aircraft were withdrawn to defend the home country.[68] During the year 200,000 tons of bombs were dropped on Germany, almost five times as much as in 1942.[69]

Before being taken on at an ordnance factory, recruits had to pass a stiff medical examination. At Glascoed Royal Ordnance Factory (Monmouthshire) during the first nine months of 1942, 2,394 men were examined and 1,106 – 45% – of them were rejected as unfit. In comparison with the First World War, such rejection was one of the factors which helped to reduce death and injury from toxic jaundice. During the period January 1943 to June 1945 just 28 cases were recorded nationally with 5 being fatal. Workers' health was further helped when dental and chiropody services were introduced.[70]

A day nursery had been established at the Bishop's Palace in 1942,[71] yet a survey of the available places in nurseries and crèches conducted in April 1943, revealed that only half had been taken up.[72]

A Ministry of Labour survey on absenteeism found that that of women was twice that of men, and that of married women was significantly higher again, highlighting the difficulties women had in juggling home and working lives.[73] By 1943 7.5 million women were in paid employment in the UK, 1.5 million of them in essential industries. The number in engineering had grown by a factor of six since 1939, up from 100,000 to 600,000. Perhaps surprisingly, but indicating the depth of the 1930s recession, it was not until 1943 that Britain reached full employment.[74] By 1943 90% of single and 80% of married women were engaged in some form of war work.[75] The 'conscription of grandmothers' – women up to the age of 50 – was brought in during the year.[76]

Filling of 500lb bombs at Rotherwas was done by a team of four who were expected to fill 12 bombs during their eight hour shift. The checker, the senior of the four, was responsible at the start of the shift for collecting 12 detonators from the isolated detonator store, carrying them in a cardboard box lined with cotton wool. The checker was always accompanied by a security guard whose job was to keep other people well away and open doors to ensure that no-one accidentally bumped into her. The girls filling the bombs worked on a raised platform with the bomb stood upright in front of them. First a black, tar-like substance was poured in and allowed to cool before liquid TNT was added. This TNT was liquefied on site from solid TNT broken down with a wooden mallet. A weighed out amount of amatol – similar to soapflakes in substance – was then added and hand-stemmed – compacted for a set period of time using a wooden stave very similar to a broomstick before two more volumes of amatol were added and stemmed, after which the exploder, trytol, was added. The final layer was more liquid TNT poured in around a former to produce the space into which the primer and fuze would later be screwed. Once all the fillings had been added the bomb was sealed with black tar.[77] Fuzing of munitions was carried out at the point in time just before they were to be used – the firing of an artillery shell or the loading of a bomb into an aircraft.

4,000 tons of new storage for filled munitions became available at Hayes Wood Quarry, Wiltshire in May 1943 at a cost of £48,000. This was said to be cheaper than that at Pontrilas. Hayes Wood also served Bridgend and Glascoed.[78]

Mr. Parsons the Chief Billeting Officer resigned in December and the council advertised the post offering a salary of £250 for a male, or £175 for a female. The job went to Mrs. C.M. Lloyd.[79]

The Allies spent the early part of 1944 preparing for the Normandy landings in June. The bombing campaign concentrated not just on industrial Germany but also on destroying the rail network the Germans would need to bring up reinforcements with an ever increasing monthly tonnage of bombs being dropped. During February the USAAF made 13 raids which crippled German aircraft production, losing 210 bombers and 38 fighters in the process. Meanwhile Bomber Command started to use the 12,000lb Tallboy bomb that was capable of displacing a million tons of earth, in one case to destroy the Saumur railway tunnel; the RAF's Lancaster carried a heavier bomb load than did the American B17 Flying Fortress. During the period before D Day the RAF flew 71,800 sorties and dropped 94,200 tons of bombs, compared to the USAAF's Eighth and Ninth Air Forces' 123,600 missions which dropped 101,200 tons of bombs. The raids also caused huge attrition to German aircraft and pilots. As these raids continued, more and more men were withdrawn from British industry to serve in the armed forces.[80]

By this time the Ammunition Supply Depots had grown enormously, with some holding more than 100,000 tons of munitions. The factories or ports (for imported munitions) despatched new munitions to the Central Ammunition Depots to fill deficiencies in the strategic reserves or to one of the Ammunition Supply Depots. If possible, issues were made from Ammunition Supply Depots which had fewer facilities to deal with faulty munitions and only in cases of exceptional demand did withdrawals come from the Central Ammunition Depots. Storage conditions at the Ammunition Supply Depots were not of the best. The one at Loch Lomond held 65,000 tons of ammunition including half a million rounds of totally obsolete, 18 pdr shells. The commanding officer complained that a shortage of fencing had allowed cattle into the site and that they had even eaten tarpaulins covering live ammunition. At Olney (Hampshire) an officer and eight men were killed when they were emptying mines, and a complete ammunition train containing surplus ammunition blew up, killing eight and injuring many more at the Savenake Forest depot in Wiltshire. But the biggest explosion happened on 27 November 1944 when 15,000 tons of ammunition exploded in one of the underground storage depots at Fauld (Staffordshire). Eighty-one people were killed and a huge crater was formed. Enormous quantities of munitions were issued in the days leading up to D Day and in the weeks after; so much so that the Home Guard were brought in to help. 1,100 wagon loads of munitions passed through Thingley Junction in Wiltshire in the 13 days following D Day.[81]

The allied bombing campaign led to a colossal demand for bombs and it may have been this pressure which led to the massive explosion which occurred at Rotherwas on 30 May, the biggest explosion at any of the Second World War filling factories. The factory at the time was employing around 2,700 people – 2,000 of them women[82] – and some 800 were on duty at the time of the explosion. Unit 6 on the Southern Section was filling 2,000lb bombs and naval mines when a bomb which was cooling after filling before being sealed, was seen to be smoking.[83] The fire alarm was immediately sounded but it required verbal confirmation in at least one unit (No 2), many thinking it was just another practice.[84]

Three men working in Unit 5, J.W. Little, F.J. Tyler and A.G. Morris, immediately tried to damp down the smoking bomb with sand and water. They were soon joined by six factory firemen and their joint efforts delayed the first explosion for long enough to allow most of the workers to reach their air raid shelters. The bomb on fire finally split open and then at around 6 p.m. exploded, killing Mr. Morris. Assistant Fire Brigade Officer F.A. Lewis in charge of the firemen was blown out of the filling house, and when he returned he found several other bombs had been set on fire. He and his crew tried desperately to put out the fire and to cool the damaged bombs but sometime between 6.45 and 7 p.m. a second, major explosion occurred and the building collapsed on those fighting the fire and other rescuers. By now the fire brigade from Hereford was assisting and help was arriving from local army bases – British, American and Canadian.

There was a third, lesser explosion and following this the fires were gradually brought under control. In all, the equivalent of 31 2,000lb bombs and mines exploded, yet by 8 p.m. the fire was brought under control.[85] Amazingly, there were just the two deaths.

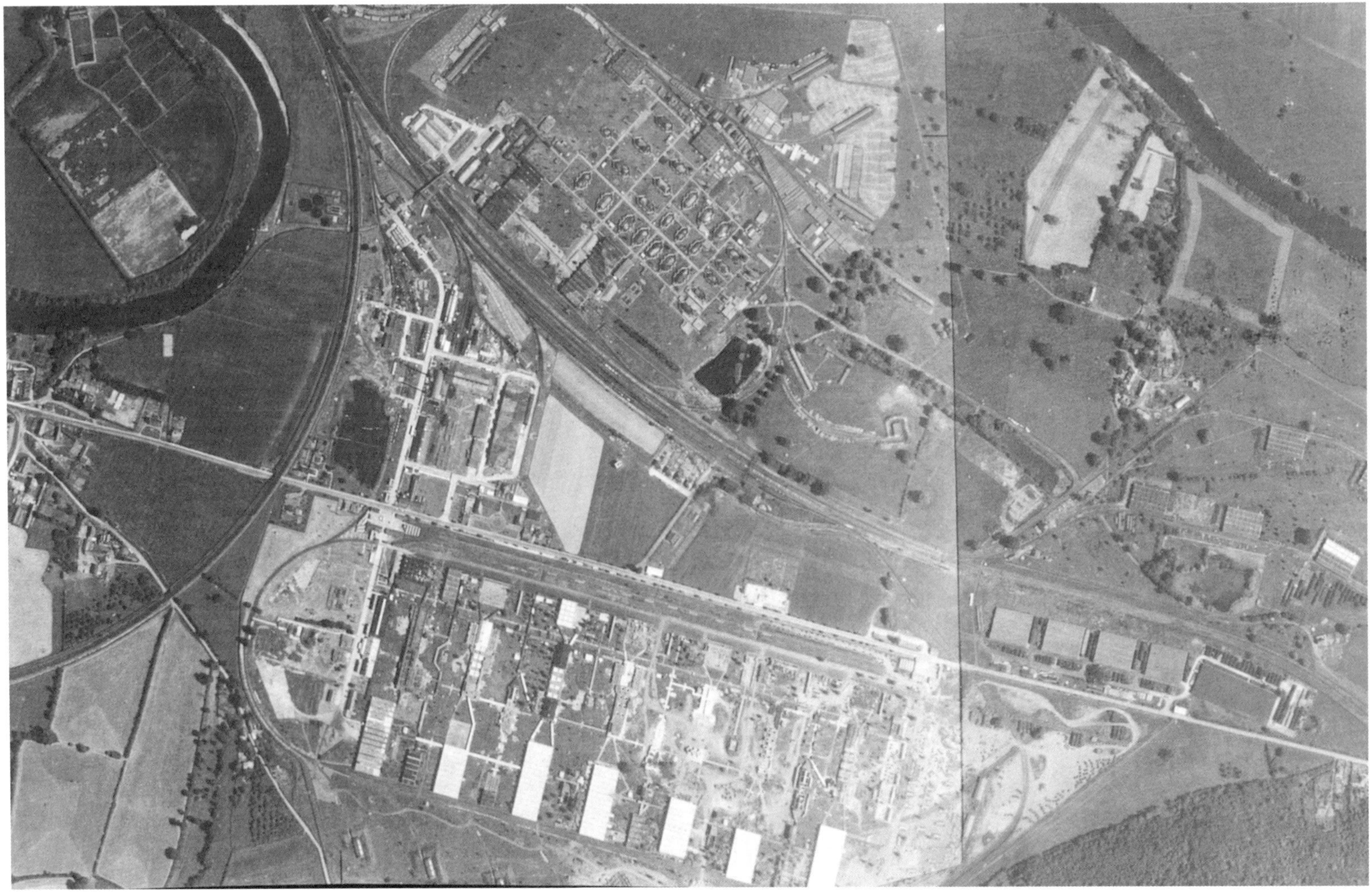

An expert with a very complete knowledge of explosives suggests that the explosive force of the second major explosion was much reduced because the bombs and mines were not fully sealed. He stated that had the munitions been fully operational a great deal more of the factory would have disappeared and perhaps much of the surrounding area.[86] As it was, an area approaching 400 by 350 yards was almost totally devastated, with damage to roofs extending over much of the Southern Section.[87]

Extensive but minor damage was also caused beyond the factory. Most houses near to the site had their windows blown in,[88] and shops in Hereford city centre were still claiming for damaged plate glass windows as late as 1947 because replacement supplies only became available then. The most distant points at which a claim was accepted was in Whitecross Road, just short of 2.5 miles from the epicentre of the explosion, and Aylestone Hill.[89] The explosion was felt in Didley, more than six miles away.[90]

Left: Two RAF photographs of July 1946 pieced together, showing that much of the damage caused by the explosion in May 1944 has been cleared, whilst new roofing (shown in white) covers many buildings in the Southern Section. Since the 1941 photograph a small building, the detonator house, almost totally surrounded with earth traverses and served by a new rail link has been built to the east of the Northern Section. The outlines of First World War filling and melt houses are visible to the west of the rebuilt Northern Section. The four Second World War stores have been completed, bv   Romney huts have yet been erected (NMR Film No. 106G   ˀ˃ Frames 3264 and 3266)

After the first explosion, when the first casualties were incurred, an appeal was broadcast over the PA system for stretcher bearers. This was quickly answered by those who had received basic First Aid training. They were actually inside the filling house when the second explosion took place. One of their number was killed, another received a fractured skull and others had limbs and ribs broken. Mona Crawthorne, one of those who was injured, later received a letter of commendation from the Director-General of Filling Factories. Casualties were taken to the County Hospital in Hereford.[91]

Mrs. Lewis and Mrs. Hughes, aged six and eight in 1944, are the daughters of the factory's then senior electrician and they lived in one of the two cottages next to the coach house, formerly part of the Rotherwas House estate buildings. The first explosion found them picnicking with their mother down river from Rotherwas. They immediately returned home. They had just entered into their house when the second explosion occurred. All the windows in the cottage were blown in, the curtains tattered and their father, one of those transferred from Woolwich in 1941, who was in the bath was badly cut by flying glass. He insisted on going back on duty and found workers fleeing past their cottage and wading to safety across the river to Hampton Park. When the original alarm had sounded these people had gone as in training exercises to their designated air raid shelter, but had panicked with the force of the second explosion.[92]

Mrs. Carmichael, who had started work at Rotherwas in 1934, was working as a checker in Unit 2 where un-rotating projectiles (the explosive part of anti-aircraft rockets) were being filled. She took cover in one of the roadside air raid shelters on the far side of the earth traverse from where the explosion took place, but had just reached it when she said the wall 'hit' her when the major explosion occurred. She hurriedly left the shelter and ran home to Rylands Street, a distance of about 2.5 miles, without stopping. She noticed damage to buildings on the way home.[93]

Mrs. Ann Edwards was a baby at the time of the explosion living with her parents in Firemans Row. She was told that all the houses were evacuated as soon as the second explosion occurred.[94]

Buried under the thousands of tons of rubble were at least 900 tons of explosives made up of partially filled munitions and high explosives in various states of preparation. The range of filled ammunition went from 25lb shells to naval mines, the latter containing as much as a ton of high explosive, and 2,000lb bombs. All was left well alone by the factory staff until W.L. Fitzmaurice from the Headquarters of the Technical Staff arrived on 5 June to take charge of making the area safe. The job took a full month. The most difficult part was the removal of 1,500lb of exploders, the most sensitive explosive on site. They were

The devastation of the May 1944 explosion was recorded in a painting by Ruskin Spear, now in the possession of the Imperial War Museum. To the left are probably the remains of three incorporating roller mills and on the centre right, what is left of one or more of the transit sheds. On the extreme right is the ruins of what had been the mess room / canteen on the north side of the Holme Lacy road. The view is towards the west and it is thought that the viewpoint is perhaps 100 yards to the west of the epicentre of the explosion. (IWM LD5636)

> ROYAL ORDNANCE FACTORY, HEREFORD
>
> To: Miss M.E. Cawthorne,
> "Audley"
> Redhill Hostel,
> Hereford.
>
> I am happy to inform you that for your devotion to duty on the occasion of the explosions on 30th May, 1944, you have received recognition.
>
> The Director General will announce particulars of the recognition in the West Satellite Canteen at 4.30p.m. on Tuesday, 9th January, 1945.
>
> Seating accommodation has been reserved for you and for 2 relatives or friends. Please arrange to be in your seats not later than 4.15p.m.
>
> The names of the 2 relatives or friends should be communicated by you personally to Police Headquarters, War Department Constabulary, R.O.F. Hereford not later than 5.0p.m. on Monday, 8th January, 1945.
>
> After the announcements, you are invited to tea with your 2 relatives or friends in Central Office Mess Room.
>
> You are granted special leave with pay for your whole shift on Tuesday, 9th instant.
>
> R. Digby Owens
> Superintendent,
> R.O.F. Hereford.
>
> 3rd January, 1945
> RVT

Mona Cawthorne was in the Mechanised Transport Corps working at Rotherwas, her duties including transporting munitions. On 9 January 1945 the Director-General, C.S. Robinson presented Miss Cawthorne with a letter commending her for her actions transporting injured people to hospital despite being hurt herself during the second explosion in May 1944

contained within boxes, many of which were broken or crushed in a completely wrecked building. The debris was never allowed to dry out being dampened by a continuous spray of water.[95]

The *Hereford Times* reported the explosion the following week, using its usual euphemism as 'happening at a West Country Royal Ordnance Factory'. The report adds details such as that the city cinema had been evacuated because it was thought that a bomb had been dropped, and that the resulting column of smoke could be seen for miles around with hundreds of relatives of the workers rushed to the factory seeking news of their kinfolk. The report ends with the statement that an inquest would be held in due course – but no report of it appeared in the paper.[96]

In January 1945 censorship was relaxed allowing the first detailed report of the 1944 explosion to appear, this in the *London Gazette* of 5 January 1945. It was followed by an in-depth report in the *Hereford Times* of 13 January 1945. This listed the five George Medals, the OBE, the MBE and the nine British Empire Medals awarded and the 34 other commendations given out. The medals were presented by the king at Buckingham Palace and the other awards handed out in a ceremony in one of the factory canteens.[97]

Other than reports about the explosion, little information about activities at Rotherwas during 1944 has been found. No attempt was made to repair the damaged buildings and many of those working at Rotherwas were transferred to other Royal Ordnance factories. Mr. Edward Thomas, an inspector who had begun work at Rotherwas in 1938, went to Kirby (Lancashire), only returning to his family in Hereford about a year after the war ended.

The war in Europe ended in May 1945 and that against Japan in August, with Britain a much impoverished nation. Some 12% of all the country's capital assets were destroyed between 1940 and 1945.[98]

During the Second World War, Royal Ordnance Factory No 4, Hereford produced

24,737,000	25 pdr high explosive shells.
2,117,000	3 inch mortar bombs
17,881,000	35 pdr quick firing cartridges
2,259,000	3.7 inch anti-aircraft cartridged shells

plus aerial bombs, naval mines, depth charges, torpedoes and rockets.[99]

Rotherwas exceeded the shell production per employee at all the other Royal Ordnance Factories and produced shells, mines, bombs and depth charges. At its peak the factory had employed 8,000 people. Together with Bridgend and Glascoed, it formed the Western Region of the Royal Ordnance Factories.

8 Wartime Accommodation Developments in Hereford

On 23 May 1939 the Land Agent of Western Command, Chester, wrote to his superior, the Chief Land Agent in London giving details of a site for a Militia hutted camp site that was to became Bradbury Lines, later renamed as Stirling Lines when the Special Air Services took it over. Associated with Bradbury Lines was the provision of housing for married quarters, construction of which continued over a long period.

The site forms part of a triangular area bounded by the Ross Road to the west, the former GWR railway line to Abergavenny to the south and the Holme Lacy Road and Hoarwithy Road to the north and east. Internally a smaller triangle is made by the Ross road, the railway and Bullingham Lane and this contained a partially built housing estate at the time of the purchase. The site was already provided with sewage and a 4 inch water main, with approval from the city council for a further 104 houses. The purchase of much of this area from three Hereford owners seems to have gone though without too many problems although the acquisition of the partially developed housing estate resulted in a voluminous correspondence. The housing estate was developed, almost certainly as a speculative venture, by Messers. McConnel of Oldham but at the time of the purchase by the War Department the District Bank of Manchester had foreclosed. The estate consisted of 80 semi-detached houses of which 44 were on the east side of Ross Road, between Bullingham Lane and the railway, eight were on the south side of Bullingham Lane, with the remainder in Red Hill Avenue and Bailey Brook Road.

The District Bank at first tried to impose conditions on the sale but were quickly informed that having turned down the offer made by the Chief Land Agent and Valuer, the site was to be acquired by the War Department using their compulsory powers and no conditions could be imposed. This dispute did not delay the War Department beginning work on the site after taking possession early in June 1939. The District Bank switched tack and tried to obtain extra payments by suggesting that the news that a military camp was to be built nearby had either made houses difficult to let or impossible to sell. Again the War Department was unmoved and made no additional payment.[1]

Further to the east, War Department development took place in a small area formed by Hoarwithy Lane, the Holme Lacy Road and the other, eastern end of Bullingham Lane. Quite what was built here remains unclear but anecdotal evidence has been obtained to suggest that War Department, flat-roofed, houses were built some time before 1941 in Manor Road.[2] Aconbury Avenue, running off Manor Road, was where five Royal Ordnance Factory married police quarters were built in 1941 and 1942. Later, War Department Constabulary quarters were added.[3] Today the whole of these areas, with the exception of Stirling Lines itself are fully developed. Build quality of the wartime housing here is poor.

Some of the houses were rented out to skilled workers, many of whom came from Woolwich where the labour force was being reduced.[4] The Ministry of Supply owned the cottages near to Rotherwas Chapel and these too were used to house workers.[5]

In June 1945 came Release Day when demobilisation began. Bradbury Lines became one of many centres where service men and women entered and civilians left. Later in the year it became the place where the army trained their mechanics to use machine tools.

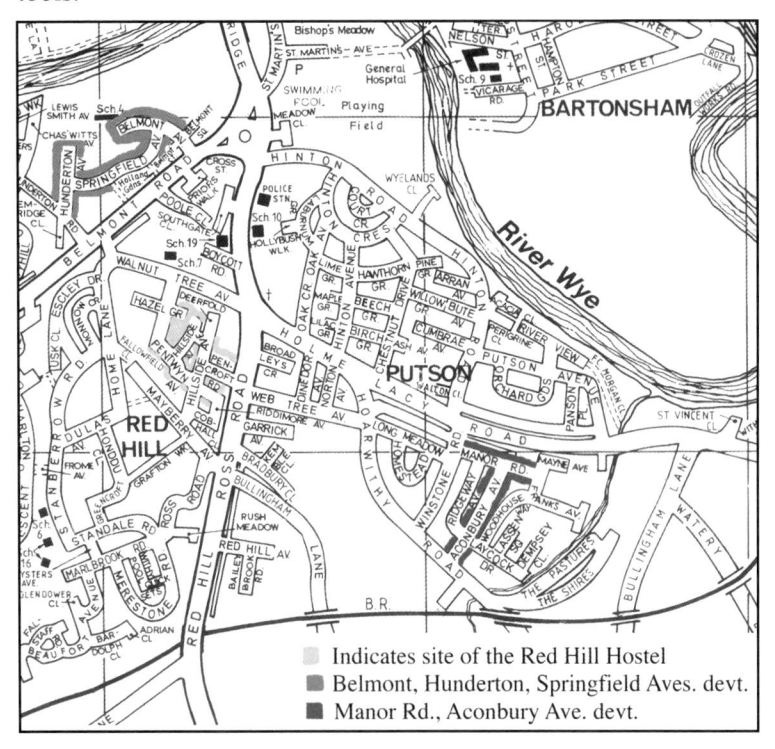

Map showing the sites of the various housing developments covered in this chapter

The Red Hill Hostel

A letter to Hereford City Council dated 16 August 1940, and strangely emanating from the Ministry of Transport in Birmingham, is the earliest indication that a hostel to house workers from the factory was under consideration. The hostel was built in 1941 with the first occupants taking up residence in May with completion of the accommodation for 2,000 people in July. The hostel was built on land on the west side of Ross Road and running back towards what is today Hazel Grove. It consisted of 20 accommodation blocks each just over 231 feet long and containing 100 sleeping cubicles. Separating these 20 blocks into two groups were the dining and the recreation centres. To the north were the chapel and the sick bay. The area was fenced in – anecdotal evidence tells of climbing in over the fence when coming back after curfew time[6] – and it had two gatekeeper's huts which were manned 24 hours a day.

It was run on behalf of the Royal Ordnance Factories by the Holiday Fellowship, as were all such hostels nationwide[7] and they employed a staff of 180 of whom 40 were part time.[8] As with most hostels it was never over popular and failed to achieve occupancy records of greater than 70%, despite also providing accommodation for Land Army girls and other government, and later private, employees. With the ending of the war the buildings were handed over to the city council to manage on 4 May 1948, and for some time continued to be used as a hostel.[9] At the end of 1954 the city council began to negotiate to buy the hostel from the Ministry of Supply, the ministry asking for £350,000 – the then equivalent of the cost of building it. The sale was completed in

September 1955 at a price of £30,000 when some 270 people were living there, some resident since it opened. Rent for a single man was 52s. 6d. (£2.63) and for women and OAPs 49s. (£2.45). Parts of the site were sold off soon after the council bought the hostel, but the rest remained in use for a number of years. Neil Hirst, an employee of British Thompson Houston Company, which later became Thorn Lighting, was initially billeted there in 1956 and threatened to immediately give up his job if he wasn't quickly found better accommodation.[10] But despite such reactions to the quality of the accommodation it was only finally closed in the late 1960s with the site sold for housing, the area now occupied by the houses in Pencroft Road, Riddmore Avenue, Hillside Avenue and Cobhall Close.

The hostel's entertainment block remained in use for a while after the hostel was closed, being described in the *Hereford Times* in 1948 as the finest concert hall in the city.[11]

Housing in Belmont, Hunderton and Springfield Avenues
The final development was of a total of 100 houses and 100 flats in Belmont, Springfield and Hunderton Avenues for which the plans were submitted to the city council on 6 June 1941. This land is low lying and had been all but bypassed by the city's own early 1930s development in Hunderton Road. It also lies further away from the factory than then other suitable areas, but development of the latter would have taken good agricultural land out of production. The city council received a letter from a firm of architects, Jellicoe, acting for the Ministry of Supply, informing them that there was an intention to build houses on the site which could be of value to the city after the war. The plans for the estate, stated to be for 150 houses, sent to the city included an artist's illustration of how they would look if the flat roof design was to be replaced by a pitched roof, and if the ARP bricks partially covering the windows were removed. The estate was built by Griggs and Sons Ltd. who had their offices at the Red Hill Hostel, and Jellicoe appointed Laurence Fermaud as their resident architect.

The City Surveyor wrote asking for better quality materials to be used, but was quickly told that the need was to build the houses using as little labour as possible. All but two pairs of semi-detached houses survive, with around half now converted to a pitched roof. All the houses are constructed with a small entry

Flat-roofed houses built in 1941 in Belmont Avenue

porch built from concrete slabs jutting out some 18 inches from the wall. For the semi-detached houses these formed the front entrance with the door surrounded by glass bricks, providing light to the hall. The porch is also a feature of the lower floor flats where it houses the window of the bathroom, and entry is via a door on the end wall. Once built, the houses were let on individual tenancies with the occupiers being responsible for rates. In 1942 the Ministry provided each house or flat with a garden shed and the estate was completed by the end of July that year. With the influx of families came the provision of day nurseries in 1942/43 at Whitecross and St. Martins. Later still came the building of Hunderton School at the west end of Belmont Avenue which was completed in 1944.[12]

In February 1945 the Town Clerk suggested that Hereford's population had returned to near pre war figures, but at the same time J.P.L. Thomas, Hereford's M.P., appealed for more lodgings. A new housing estate to the west of the Ministry of Supply Springfield Avenue was planned, whilst in May 1946 an attempt by squatters to take over parts of Bradbury Lines was thwarted by the Ministry of Defence Police.

Having 103 applications for homes on their books during the late 1940s the council also approached the Ministry of Supply to take over the Belmont Avenue housing estate but they turned them down. In November 1954 discussions began again as the ministry now wanted to sell the estate, a sale which eventually went through. During the 1980s and 1990s many of the houses were bought by the sitting tenants.

Fireman's Row
To the east of the main development in the Central Section of the factory six semi-detached and one detached houses were built as part of the 1930s redevelopment. They were used to house part of the resident fire fighting force.

Flat-roofed houses in Hunderton Avenue from the rear

9   The Change to Civilian Use[1]

Rotherwas Royal Ordnance Factory was officially closed on 29 September 1945. On 20 September many of those working at site had been given notice terminating their employment[2] and by the end of the month the numbers employed by the Ministry of Supply was down to 1,500. A deputation from the remaining workforce visited Philip Warter, Controller General of Factories and Storage Premises to the Board of Trade, to try to get the closure reconsidered. On their return, the chairman of Hereford Trades Council said that they had failed and that many other ordnance factories were closing their filling activities. As part of the reorganization, Digby Ovens, the former factory manager, was promoted to control all the Ministry of Supply storage depots in Herefordshire, the Forest of Dean and South Wales, the ministry then using part of the site to break down tanks and bren gun carriers.[3] Later they were to use the site for the auctioning of surplus stores and for the assembly of gas masks. The last day of 1949 saw a presentation to Digby Ovens, retiring after 28 years as factory superintendent. The day before he had been lauded by the workers and the Trade Unions.

It wasn't long before the chairman of Hereford's Town Planning Committee, H.F.B. Biggs, wrote to the Ministry of Supply asking them to put pressure on the Ministry of Defence to release buildings for industrial use. It was certainly very shortly after the end of the war that some buildings were identified as available for private industrial use.[4]

The Ministry of Defence began their breaking-down operation setting aside land on the eastern edge of the Southern Section. An employee there was charged with stealing bearings from a bren carrier but the case was dismissed when the defence proved them to have come from the gear box of a Cromwell tank! A crane driver was killed in 1947 at what was then called the Directorate Disposal of Breakdown Unit. In February 1949 it was announced that half of the employees engaged in breaking-down tanks were to be discharged and that the breaking-down operation would end in June when the site would become solely a Ministry of Supply storage depot, with the remaining work being transferred to Nottingham. Those employed at Rotherwas then learnt that workers at the Pontrilas munitions depot, who mostly lived in Wales, were provided with subsidized travel. Their requests for comparable treatment were noted but not acted upon. The changes at Rotherwas took place more slowly than expected and in March the *Hereford Times* stated that the reductions in the Ministry of Supply workforce would not be complete until September.

Evidence for the existence of the breaking down operation was found when Arctic Gold began building their factory in the 1990s at the eastern end of the Southern Section – two tank periscopes and a number of tank engine parts were unearthed.[5] The county council also recovered tank pieces, digging up a number of tracks when building roads in this eastern area.[6]

The change to sole use as a storage depot and auction site if anything increased the level of activity. An aerial photograph

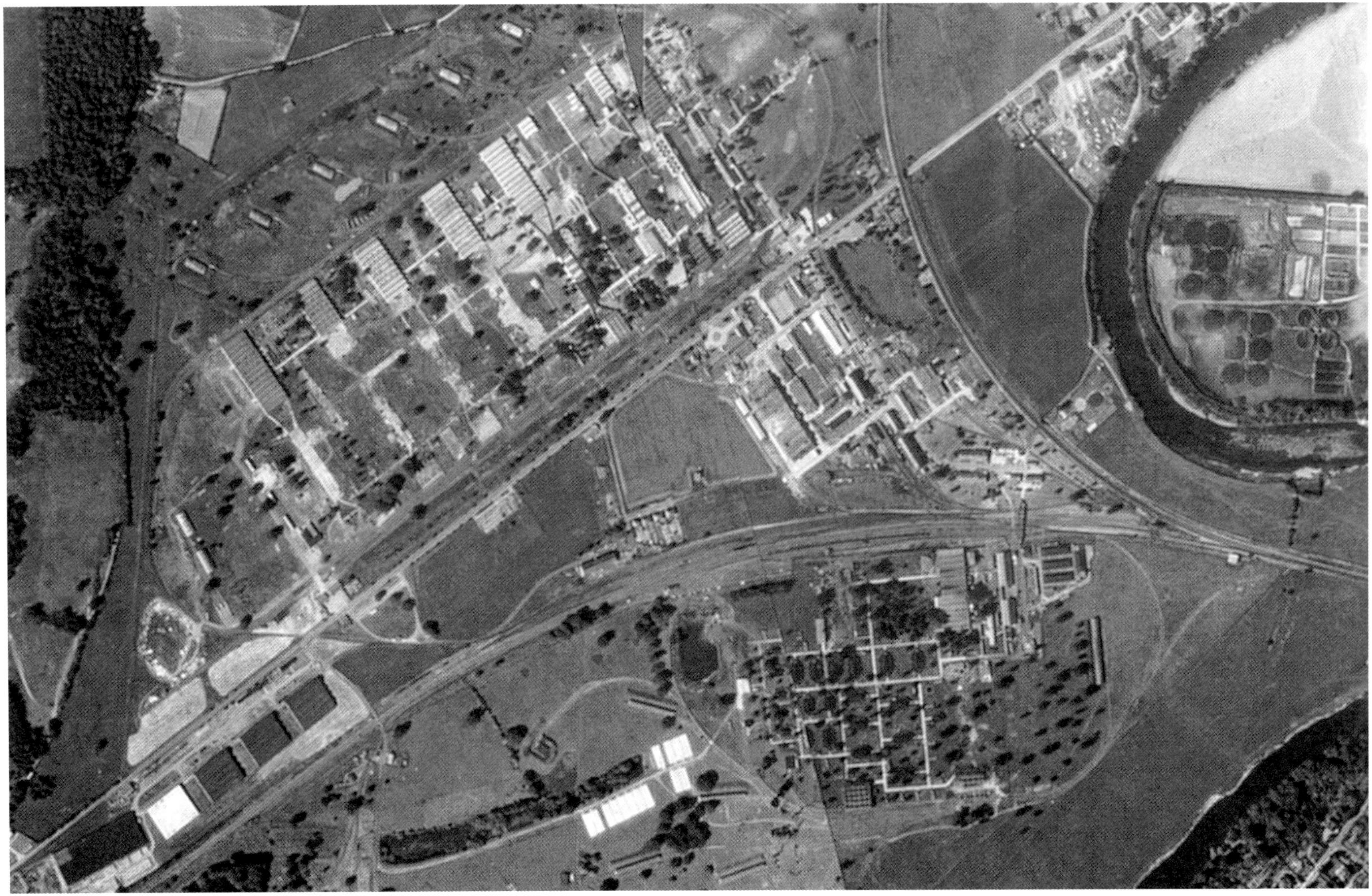

Left: An aerial photograph of June 1961. The eastern empty shell store in the Northern Section has gone, but all the buildings to the west of the other empty shell store remain intact. Considerable tree growth has occurred, most if not all of the internal railway has been taken up but the line to Ross-on-Wye remains open. Above: Aerial photograph in 1998 with the Wye in flood, bottom left, reaching the edge of the picric acid bond store. Trees and undergrowth have recently been cleared on the Northern Section

dated 11 July 1946 (see page 74) shows items stacked near most of the buildings on the site.[7]

The first of the many auction sales held by the Ministry of Supply at Rotherwas, all conducted by Messers. Russell, Baldwin and Bright, took place over 16 to 19 November 1948. The goods sold were a very mixed collection of items including 100 motor vehicles, 10,000, 10 and 20 inch rubber tyred bogey wheels and radios. A sale in August 1953 included for the first time items described as being held at places other than Rotherwas. Usually held every three months, in February, May, August and November, the sales were to continue until June 1962 when they were transferred to Moreton-on-Lugg. A 1961 aerial photograph shows that the storing of goods outside had ceased, and that the Romney huts had been erected. This suggests that these are second hand and brought in from elsewhere.[8]

A section of the factory was abandoned late in 1956, probably most of the Northern Section, and the county council, concerned at rising levels of unemployment, wanted to acquire the land in order to attract new firms to the city. The council then formed an Industrial Development Committee in March 1958, reacting to rumours that the depot at Rotherwas was to be bulldozed and the land returned to agriculture. In response to enquiries, the Ministry of Supply stated that some buildings might be available for release, adding that a review of the site was being undertaken.

The first firm known to have established themselves on the Rotherwas estate was Harcourt & Co. Ltd., the production side of the Hotpoint Electrical Co. Ltd. They set up business in part of the Central Section either in 1945 or 1946. Starting in 1946 and continuing over a four year period, correspondence to and from to the Water Pollution Research Laboratory details the measures taken to prevent a poisonous discharge of sodium cyanide from the firm's plating shop into the River Wye.[9] That these problems were serious was proven when polluted soil down to a depth of 16 feet had to be dug out during a 1970s refurbishment.[10] The plating shop together with the press shop, the metal finishing and paint shop were housed in a large 1930s building, home during the war to the Civilian Inspectorate of Ammunition. This building was demolished in 1981. In March 1949 it was announced that Harcourts were to amalgamate with Edison Swan Electric Ltd. and that the workforce would be increased. Harcourts were then employing 142 men and 116 women and the prospect was that these figures would rise to 180 and 350 respectively. The Mayor and his council toured the Edison Swan factory at Rotherwas in 1951. They saw fluorescent lighting being made for Turkish mines and Dutch railways, together with kettle manufacture. Harcourts became the Edison Swan Electric Co. Ltd. in 1950, British Thompson Houston Co. Ltd. in 1957, British Lighting Industries Ltd. some time in the 1970s and finally Thorn Lighting Ltd. before closing on 31 December 1999. They occupied most of the Central Section and at some time part of either Unit 1 or 2 on the Southern Section.[11]

On 30 September 1948 Messes. Sankey and Sons Ltd. of Bilston, Staffordshire, leased one of the empty shell stores and ancillary buildings on the Southern Section totalling 43,000 square feet where they began to produce stainless steel beer barrels. In 1955 they moved into the production of tubular chairs but closed their whole factory in April 1972.

A railway map *circa* 1950 shows George Cohen Ltd. based on the Northern Section undertaking the same job as they did after the First World War at Credenhill, namely breaking down ammunition. Nationally, disposal of all of the Second World War ammunition was not completed until 1964.[12] Cohen's are shown as using the western empty shell store as their headquarters,[13] the eastern empty shell store being demolished some time between 1946 and 1961.[14] At some time during the 1950s the firm began to bring in old rolling stock from the London Underground for breaking down.[15]

In 1950 further land was released by the Ministry of Supply for industrial development. Exactly what these areas were has not been discovered but it is thought that it may have included two AOD stores plus the one which burnt down. These are today privately owned.

In August 1956 the Ministry of Supply announced that they were dismissing or redeploying all 200 people employed in their gas mask assembly unit. Of those to go 141 women and 24 were men with the remainder being transferred to other jobs. The assembly unit, which had been in operation since 1950, had been controlled from the Glascoed Royal Ordnance Factory. There was no question, however of an overall closure of the depot. The women were all local and had earned around £6 per week. The Labour Exchange thought that the chances of them finding new jobs was fairly remote, but British Thompson Houston had vacancies for between 30 and 40. When Henry Wiggin & Co. opened their new factory at Holmer to the north of the city later that year, there were further job prospects.

In 1972 the county council began negotiations with the Ministry of Defence, the department then responsible for the site, to buy the remainder of the Rotherwas site. The *Hereford Times* wrote of the vast size of many of the buildings and suggested that some could be used for indoor sports, whilst there were several transport firms only too willing to lease others. On 21 December 1973, in its last land transaction before being absorbed into the County of Hereford and Worcester, Herefordshire County Council completed the purchase.[16] In 1972 the city council had bought a small piece of the site for a new sewage works now managed by Hyder plc. The works have since been greatly extended and has meant that two picric acid stores have been demolished.

Part of the south-west corner of the Southern Section was taken over by caravan squatters in 1953. The county council was requested to get rid of them but their attempts failed and, eventually bowing to the inevitable, they made it into an officially designated gypsy site with showers and toilets available and which was inaugurated in March 1974.

The Hereford to Ross-on-Wye railway closed on 2 November 1964 together with the Barton Cross Station and engine depot, in effect isolating the Northern Section which even today lacks direct road access. In 1974 the wooden buildings within the blast walls on the Northern Section were demolished.[17]

Remains of the Munitions Factory in 2004

Today much of the Northern Section is derelict and abandoned. The western picric acid expense store and three bond stores survive, now isolated in farmland, with the later used for hay and straw storage. All of the Second World War buildings to the west of the boiler house have been cleared with the hardcore formed piled in heaps on site. The 1961 aerial photographs showed the beginnings of natural reafforestation and three decades later in 1996 a selection was made of mature trees to be retained before the others and the undergrowth were cleared. In the seven years since this clearance the undergrowth has rapidly re-grown; the relative isolation of this part of the site has allowed it to become something of a nature reserve. In 1994 a series of trial holes and trenches were dug to test for industrial pollution, the only positive findings being on the site of the railway sidings where arsenic was discovered. The area occupied in the First World War by Unit 1 and used then and perhaps again during the 1920s for charging shells with mustard gas was not examined. The possibility of demolishing and crushing the existing blast walls and cleanways and of digging the estimated 800,000 tons of sand and gravel on the site was rejected as being uneconomic.[18] As for potential redevelopment, the Department of the Environment is resisting the council's attempts to develop the Northern Section because it considers the area prone to flooding; in 1960 Thorn Lighting were reported as having lost £60,000 to this cause.

Twenty-four Z-shaped air raid shelters survive in this section, as do a number of others built on the road side of an earth traverse put in place between the wars between the Southern Section and the Holme Lacy road, with two more in the Central Section. The exterior walls are of 14 inch brickwork with a 6 inch concrete roof said to provide protection from a direct hit by an incendiary bomb

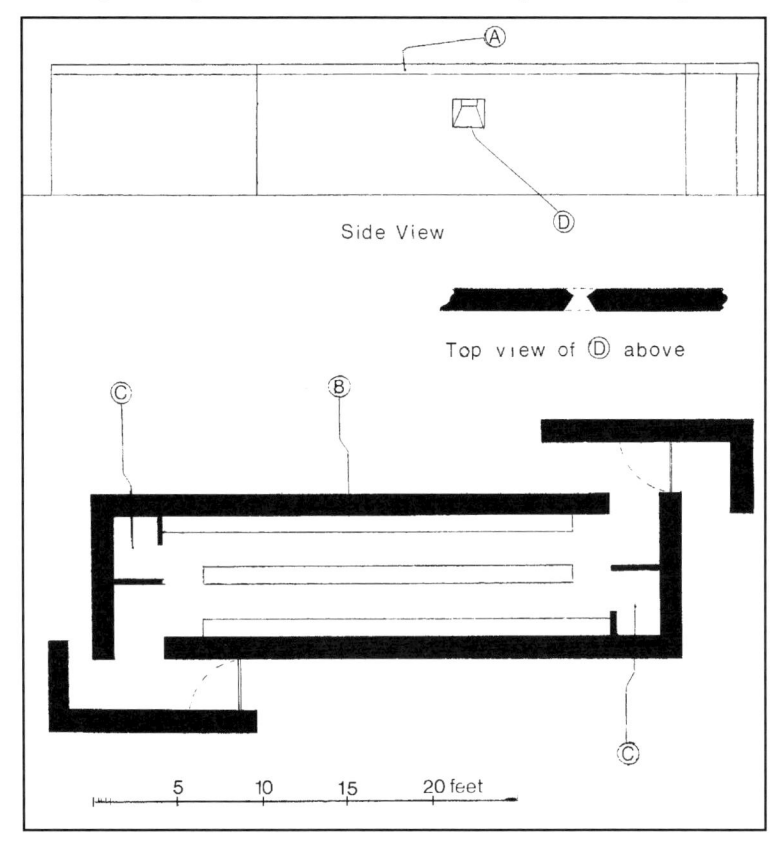

A - 6 inch cast-in-situ concrete roof covered in a layer of asphalt; B - 14 inch brick wall; C - Elsan toilet cubicles; D - Observation slit

or from a 500lb bomb exploding more than 50 yards away. These shelters were designed to accommodate around 50 people and were provided with some degree of defence against gas attacks. A sloping felt blanket could be drawn down at both entrances and when wetted would have provided a limited filtering effect. Additionally the ventilation holes set just under the roof were provided with felt covered wooden plugs. At either end is a walled off area holding an Elsan toilet indicating that longish stays were to be expected. The toilet bucket was vented to the outside. Build quality of these shelters is good with the use of bullnose rounded edge bricks at the entrances.

Plan (opposite) and photograph (above) of the interior of a Z-shaped shelter showing three rows of benching. The bench is of concrete but covered with hardboard laid on thin wooden battens. At the far end the wooden sloped support for the gas blanket is shown with the walled off toilet area to the right. A curtain could be drawn across to provide privacy

A view of one of the two underground bunkers on the Northern Section built during the inter-war reconstruction of that area. This picture was taken soon after the clearance of the undergrowth in 1997 and shows the entrance and exit for trolleys suggesting a one way traffic system. The rail access is on the other side and was fully covered (Andrew Terry, Herefordshire Council)

For no obvious reason several of the Z shelters were provided with an observation slit looking out towards the next shelter.

Shelters for the AOD stores were provided by digging a short length of tunnel into the earth traverse on the northern sides of the buildings and lining this with concrete. Only one survives.

The entrance to the only surviving underground shelter dug for the residents of the guardhouse set to the south of the southern perimeter. The capacity appears to have been about 15 and there was no defence against gas. There is anecdotal evidence of other underground shelters in the Southern Section but none survive

The Boiler House situated to the west of the western empty shell store on this section has already been described on page 57.

One of two bunkers dating from the inter-war reconstruction is used for the storage of fireworks. It was provided with rail access with space for a single wagon to be unloaded under cover. Cleanways lead into and away from the bunker suggesting one way traffic for trolleys collecting material from the store which was divided into two compartments each 20 x 18 feet in floor area. A second bunker with a much deeper covering of soil became the headquarters of the Hereford Pistol Club, but their activities were banned following the shootings at Hungerford in August 1987.

Both clean- and dirty-ways remain in place on the Northern Section, the latter recognisable by the remains of the uprights set into the kerbs which supported the roof. In the 1941 aerial photograph which was taken late in the day, it is possible to differentiate between all the clean- and dirty-ways over the whole site, the roof structure of the dirtyways producing much longer shadows. None of the extensive roadway layout on the Southern Section survives. The roadways were built to provide level access between the buildings on the site and services were carried in a trench along one side of them. They are constructed in concrete cast-in-situ and supported on concrete piers at either 8 or 12 feet intervals. All are provided with a kerb, and the roadway itself and the kerb are covered in a 1 inch layer of asphalt to make for ease in keeping them clean, and dust and rubbish free. The 1941 aerial photograph clearly shows the strict attention paid to keeping down the vegetation over the whole of the site at Rotherwas.

Cleanways on the Northern Section are of three widths: 12, 8 and 7 feet with cut away corners at 45 degrees where they join at right angles, to assist in turning a trolley. The access to the wooden working buildings set within the concrete blast walls was via a cleanway of 7 feet in width.

Three sizes of working buildings were constructed, 16 of the largest, eight medium and one small. The buildings were all wooden and were removed in 1974. A study of the plans of a number of other Royal Ordnance Filling Factories suggest that the asymmetric layout of these buildings at Rotherwas is unusual. Even in the First World War the norm was to have a standard

A length of 8 feet wide cleanway showing the supports used to produce a completely level overall complex. The corners were cut back at 45 degrees to make for ease of access

A view looking east along the most southerly of the 12 feet wide cleanways showing the 7 feet access was to the working buildings which would have been hidden behind the concrete blast walls

This photograph shows the differing widths of the Second World War cleanways. It is thought that the narrower ones allowed only one-way traffic (Andrew Terry, Herefordshire Council)

distance as set out in the 1875 Explosives Act between buildings, creating a symmetrical layout and which makes it relatively easy to deduce in retrospect the way in which materials were moved around the site. While several people who worked on this section can recall that brass cartridge cases were packed with the appropriate amount of cordite and then connected to pre-filled shells, none could recall exactly what was done in each building. One person recalled that the smallest of the wooden buildings was used to fill primers and perhaps igniters, and that no more than two people were allowed in it at one time.

The plan below shows the layout of one the eight medium sized buildings. Entry and exit to the building was via a porch provided with inner and outer doors. To secure the integrity of the blackout at night, entry would be made to the porch and the outer door would be pulled shut before the inner one allowing access to the building proper was opened. Access at both ends suggests a one way flow of materials. If the building had to be evacuated,

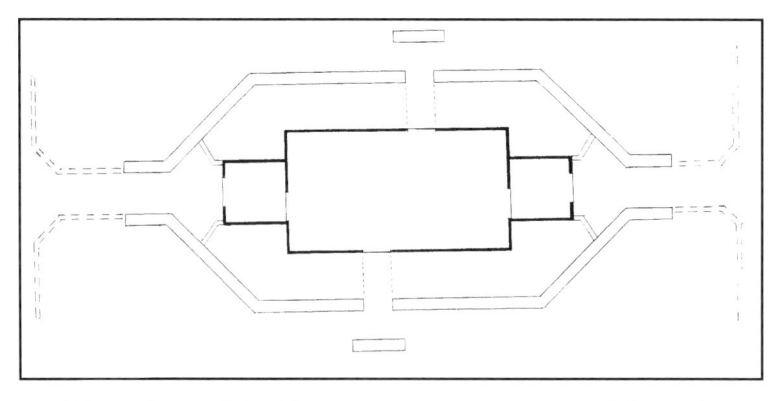

This picture, looking through one of the side 'escape' exits from a blast area, was taken during the 1997 clearance, shows on the right the undergrowth yet to be cleared. In the six years since the clearance the tree-growth has been tremendously fast and much of the North Section is once again inaccessible (Andrew Terry, Herefordshire Council)

Plan of one of the blast areas containing one of the eight medium sized buildings. All the floor area covered by the building, access to the cleanways and the escape footpath was in concrete covered in asphalt all set to the level of the cleanways. The rest of the areas enclosed by the blast walls remained unimproved and were at whatever ground level applied to the particular point. (Chatfield Collection)

A view of several of the enclosures in the north section formed by cast-in-situ concrete blast walls which surrounded the wooden working buildings of the Second World War (see also front cover). While the factory was producing munitions the whole of the surroundings would have been kept immaculately clean to ensure that nothing contaminated the explosives being handled (Andrew Terry, Herefordshire Council)

doors on the side walls provided speedy access to shelter behind the blast walls. The 16 larger buildings had two escape doors with two gaps in the blast walls.

Dating from the First World War, one expense and two bond stores for picric acid survive, the latter now used as fodder stores. Originally there were two expense and six bond stores. Each bond store was made up of 24 cell-like rooms each 5 feet wide by 7 deep and designed to store a maximum of 3,000lb of explosive, producing a overall storage capacity of just under 200 tons. The end and partition walls are in 9 inch brickwork with the front and rear walls made in wooden framing covered externally with weather boarding and internally with flat Uralite sheeting. The overall design was such as to direct the force of a possible explosion upwards and outwards away from adjoining stores.

Each of the two expense stores was divided into 32 cubicles of similar size to those of the bond stores but provided with doors at front and back to allow one way traffic. Each cubicle was provided with a drain in one corner. Two of the four windows set in both back and front walls and positioned over the doorway were louvered and could be opened. The high quality doors were hinged with brass hinges, had no latch but had a lock which could be operated either from inside or outside. Bolts were fitted to the inside only. The closing handle was a leather looped strap. When swung fully open a spring loaded catch at the top of the door was engaged to ensure that the door could not blow shut. Electric light was provided with lights shining into the cubicles from the outside of the windows. For cubicles with an odd number this was installed on the other side to that for even numbers. Anecdotal evidence states that the western expense store was used during the Second World War to disarm faulty ammunition, and certainly the absence of any from of blackout suggests daytime use only.

Each cubicle was numbered and in the First World War this was done from left to right using embossed cast iron numbers.

The west side of the picric acid expense store A wooden platform extended out some 8 feet to provide a stable unloading stage from the rail trucks parked alongside. It was supported on brick piers parts of which are still extant. Behind the brick wall in what is the left hand corner of the recess wooden brackets are evident at about 5 feet above floor level. They are thought to be supports for a fire bucket which would have been filled with sand

The surviving picric acid expense store viewed from the north east. The far end has been partially destroyed by fire. Exactly when the alterations to the roof were made is not known but originally each partition wall would have extended above the roof line as at the left

This shows the east side of the expense store complete with the only surviving remains of the First World War covered corridor. A wooden floor extended out from the cubicles at floor level and was supported to the left on cross pieces. The wall on the left is in painted corrugated iron and probably dates from the First World War

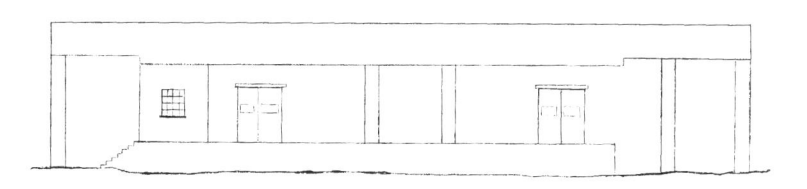

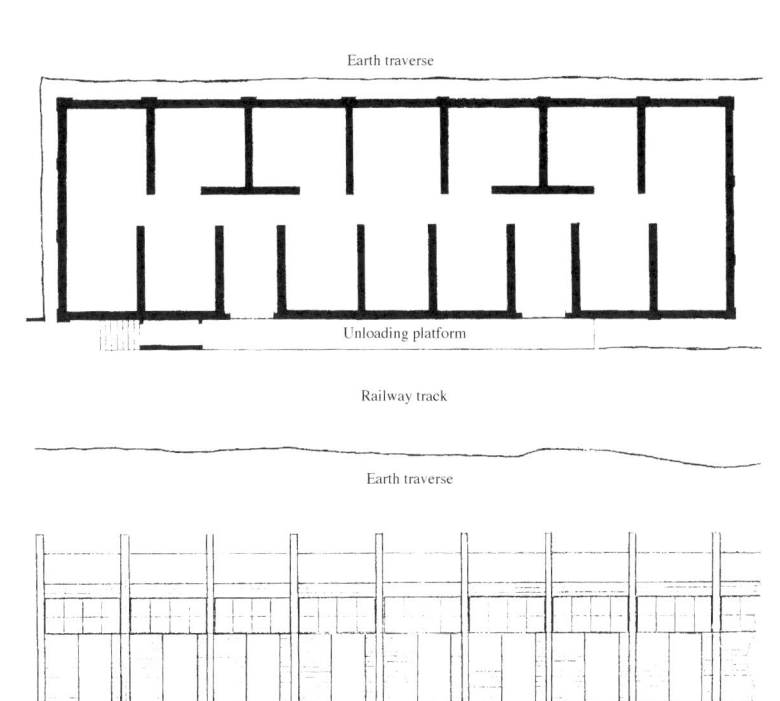

Earth traverse

Unloading platform

Railway track

Earth traverse

Top and Centre: Side elevation and plan of TNT magazine in the Southern Section
Bottom: Side elevation of a picric acid bond store

95

In the Second World War stencils were used and the numbering went from right to left but the cast iron numbers were left in place!

Deliveries of explosives via the rail link arrived to the side of the store furthest away from the lyddite factory proper. In the case of Unit 1 this was to the western side. Here a wooden platform set at rail truck floor level extended out from the store some 8 feet or so.

The western-most empty shell store on the Northern Section survives, just. Vandalism has ensured all the glass in the roof has been smashed and rain can now enter the building. It is one of two on the Northern Section of which the other has gone. Much damage was done to the seven stores on the Southern Section in the 1944 explosion. The store surviving on the Northern Section is thought to have been the first to be completed. Construction on the site began on 5 July 1916 and this building is known to have been in use by 11 November the same year. It is a 14 bay north lit shed building, a design developed in the latter part of the 19th century to allow plentiful natural light, but no direct sunlight, into the building. Each bay except the first is 25 feet wide, the first bay at 31 feet 6 inches, also containing the rail link. For an unknown reason the apex height is lower in the most northerly bay.

The building is 125 feet wide. It thus covers an area just over an acre and there are no internal uprights at all. The roof is supported at the apex on channel iron uprights, not as is more usual at the gutters. The walls are infilled with 12 inch square, hollow tile blocks with bricks used where these would be too big. Originally there were no windows but they have been added in at least two tranches and at some time or other a number of new doorways have been cut to provide egress to a number of outside buildings, most of which since been demolished.

The east side of the surviving western empty shell store in the North Section. This building is rapidly reaching the point beyond which it can be saved. Measuring 365 feet long and with an internal floor area of just over an acre, it was built in four months in 1916; construction began on 5 July and it was in use on 7 November. The curve above the RSJ in the end bay shows the position of the roof cover of the First World War exit towards the filling houses. This was the building where there were plans to charge shells with mustard gas in the late 1920s (Andrew Terry, Herefordshire Council)

The tracks inside the empty shell store used to move the shells, each marked with the maximum load allowed

Only one honesty box has survived. Here those working the internal rail system, employed by the Ministry of Munitions in the First and by the Royal Ordnance factory in the Second World Wars, were on honour bound to deposit contraband before entering any of the secure areas

Both the Northern and Southern secure areas were fenced, with entry strictly controlled. The fence between the Northern Section and the railway is thought to date from the inter war reconstruction when the fence was moved. Trains entered the secure area through wide gates and the train drivers and shunters were subject to the same rules regarding contraband as those working in the section. They wore clean white overalls and an honesty box was provided close to the entry gates. Here they were expected to deposit any contraband before entry.

Undoubtedly the most ornate building on site is the administration building, built during the First World War. At a time when labour was desperately short, small 2 inch bricks were used and a useless empty cupola added.

The ornate style of the First World War administration building is typical of many building designed by the then head of the Office of Works, Frank Baines, later knighted. The building was used as their headquarters by Thorn Lighting but has been bought and renovated to a high standard by Pontrilas Developments who also own the rest of the Central Section

This building stands alone well isolated from any nearby structure. It is situated in the central section midway between the eastern edge of the northern section and the most westerly of the AOD stores. It has no windows, was provided with metal doors and was almost totally surrounded by earth traverses. It was linked to the railway system and thought important enough to have the fire fighting main brought close. A hydrant can be seen to the right

Only a part of one of the original nine transit sheds, two on the Northern and seven on the Southern Sections, survives and is now occupied by Deyn Plastics. It was part of Unit 1. On this section all or parts of four of the empty shell stores and two of the ammonium nitrate stores which survive are in use, some reclad with modern materials, others still with their original 1917 hollow tile infill. They and many of the surviving wartime buildings pose safety problems for the future with roofs covered in corrugated asbestos. The suggestion in a 1972 *Hereford Times* leader that transport companies would be interested in leasing the empty shell stores has come true with three of the five which survive on the Southern Section home to logistics companies. The area occupied by the incorporation sheds, the press houses and most of the other buildings damaged or destroyed in the 1944 explosion have been cleared with new roads put in and modern buildings erected.

The seven associated TNT magazines to the south remain untouched, with three being used for firework storage and four holding hay and straw. The area between the southern boundary

This is the TNT magazine which served Unit 6, today used as a fodder store. On the left is a small changing cubicle with a row of coat hooks where those coming in to work would change into factory provided clothing. The cast-in-situ wall of the cutting through which the rail trucks entered can be seen further to the left. The unloading platform is covered with a 1 inch layer of asphalt

fence and the empty shell stores is let out to a local farmer as rough grazing. The 1919 map reproduced on page 14 shows stores 6 and 7 as not having their earth traverses complete and this is confirmed in the photograph from the Bustin collection on page 17. Quite what is First World War construction and what was built in the inter-war period is unclear. The walls are probably original and are built in 13 inch brickwork. This is roofed over by a 6 inch flat concrete roof carried on internal brickwork which forms bays in the interior.

Above the concrete is the typical light roof for a building holding large quantities of explosive designed to offer little resistance to the force of a possible explosion, and which is provided with four ventilators for each magazine. This suggests that it was built during the First World War, but the roof is of corrugated asbestos with the first sheets of that material not produced until 1924 and there would have been great difficulty in pouring concrete to form the ceiling with the roof in place. This begs the question of the role of vents with the concrete ceiling in place. The floor and most of the railway platform are covered with a 1 inch layer of asphalt. The roof extends over the railway platform to allow unloading in relative dryness. The magazines are surrounded on three sides by massive earth traverses.

Access to each magazine was by rail through the northern earth traverse via a cutting provided with cast in situ concrete walls. The siding serving each magazine was gated at the mid point allowing just sufficient room for a train bringing TNT to or taking it from the magazines to pull off the main loop. Anecdotal evidence states that one or more empty trucks were placed between the engine and those actually containing explosive. The engines would have been fitted with spark arrestors. During the First World War Rotherwas was supplied with three new and four second-hand standard gauge, railway locomotives, the oldest dating back to 1888. During the Second World War six new and seven second-hand locomotives were at work, the first arriving in 1937. The Pontrilas storage depot had two new and eight second-hand engines. The disposal history of all these engines is recorded.[19]

The Second World War watchtower is positioned just inside the south perimeter fence close to one of the two gates in the fence. While at first this building was thought to have been a guard tower, according to Lowery in *20th Century Defences in Britain* buildings intended to house troops defending an area or structure were always constructed in concrete because brickwork was easily destroyed by machine gun fire. This building is a brick walled structure with a cast-in-situ floor and roof. It rests on four brick pillars.

At least two pillboxes survive, both of which are Type 23 and constructed in cast-in-situ concrete. They are six-sided structures with entry on the side nearest the factory.

The Central Section was owned by Thorn Lighting who closed their operation on 31 December 1999. In the spring of 2001 the area was bought by Pontrilas Developments who own and run industrial estates elsewhere in Herefordshire, at Pontrilas and Whittington. Already the First World War hospital building next to the administration block has been cleared and a new building erected on the site where Herefordshire Council has established a machinery depot.

The poor road access to the Rotherwas Industrial Estate is a major disadvantage to firms on the estate, with the lack of headroom under the bridge carrying the railway over the Holme Lacy road and weight restrictions on Holme Lacy bridge the major problems. At least once every year an over-height lorry becomes stuck. Plans to link the new access road directly to the A49 Hereford to Ross-on-Wye, road and so avoid the bottleneck, are at an advanced stage.

In fact never officially part of the filling factory to the east of the site, five of the six Army Ordnance stores survive but all of the ten built at Credenhill have gone. Once a particular shell had been passed by the Civilian Inspectorate of Ammunition as meeting the set standards, it ceased to be the responsibility of the factory and the army took over. In practice the factory railway workers would take the shells from the transit sheds and deliver them either to the AOD stores or to designated storage elsewhere. The design of the AOD stores and of the transit sheds was similar and a first glance might suggest that it was the same as that of the

The railway loading platform for one of the AOD stores. The brick wall separating the store and the platform appears to be an addition and it may have been at this time that the gantry system which extended over the platform was removed

This was the first area of the AOD stores to be sold off and was not bought by the council. It remains in private ownership with no upgrading of the Romney huts which are at the original distance apart

empty shells stores. In fact the roof was supported at the ridge not the apex and the ridges were linked at the apex with angle iron tie rods. No reason has been found to explain this difference.

The two most easterly of the AOD stores are privately owned. One was burnt down in the 1990s and its site has recently been cleared. One of these stores retains its northern earth traverse with a passage-type air raid shelter dug into it, the only one to survive. Herefordshire Council owns the three other AOD stores and their associated Romney huts. While the AOD stores are in use, mostly for storage, the end of their useful life is in sight. However, a refurbishment programme for the council owned huts is underway. The original cladding is removed, the frame wirebrushed and repainted, and new cladding put on. These revamped units are then let as low rent starter buildings for new or smaller businesses.

The river plain of the Wye is now jealously guarded, both for its scenic qualities and as agricultural land of great value. Further downstream from Rotherwas that part of the land area enclosed by the Bartonsham bend of the river which is not used for the sewage works, land on the north side of the river at Hampton Park, and that upstream from Broomy Hill, remains undeveloped. Industrial development would be unthinkable. Without that 1916 decision to site National Filling Factory No. 14 where it was built, the Rotherwas Industrial Estate would not exist today. However, the infrastructure put during the two world wars has provided the foundation on which the county's biggest industrial estate has developed. It is home to more than 100 businesses employing around 2,000 people.

Endnotes

Chapter 1 The Background
1. Pope, Stephen and Wheal, Elizabeth Anne, *The Macmillan Dictionary of the First World War*, Macmillan, 1997. First published by Macmillan Reference Books,1995, p.85.
2. *The Times*, November 1914.
3. Cross, Robin, *World War 1 in Photographs*, Paragon, 1996, p.30.
4. Winter, Jay and Baggett, Blaine, *The Great War and the Shaping of the 20th Century*, Penguin Books., 1996, p.199.
5. Pope, Stephen and Wheal, Elizabeth Anne, *op. cit.*, p.168.
6. Taylor, A.J.P., *English History 1914–1945*, Clarendon Press, 1965. p.36.
7. Brown, I.G., *The Big Bang. A History of Explosives*, Sutton Publishing, 1998.
8. Cocroft, Wayne D., *Dangerous Energy*, English Heritage, 2000, p.168.
9. Malaws, Brian and Parry, M., *Cooke's Explosive Works*, Penrhyndeudraeth, Merioneth.
10. Brown, I.G., *op. cit.*, p.151.
11. *Ibid.*, p 153.
12. Edwards, Brian, *National Filling Factory No 5, Quedgley, Gloucester*.
13. Brown, I.G., *op. cit.*, p.159.
14. Strachen, Hew, *The Oxford Illustrated History of the First World War*, Oxford University Press, 1998, pp.259/260.
15. Spiers, Edward M., *Chemical Warfare*, Macmillan, 1986, p.47.
16. Haber, L.F., *The Poisonous Cloud. Chemical Warfare in the First World War*, Clarendon Press, 1986, p.165 onwards.
17. *Ibid.*
18. *Ibid.*
19. History of the Ministry of Munitions PRO 940/5342 Vol 8, Part 1, p.51.
20. Miall, Stephen, *A History of the British Chemical Industry*, Ernest Benn, 1931, p.85.
21. SUPP 6/622. Gas Charging Reports 1 to 10. Report No 8 Hereford.
22. Imperial War Museum, *Women at War* Archive produced between 1915 and 1921. Accessed via a series of microforms held by the Library at the University of Birmingham, D639.W.7. Reels 73 & 74.
23. *Ibid.*
24. Dewey, Peter, *War and Progress 1914–1945*, Longman, 1997.
25. Marwick, Arthur, *The Deluge*, Macmillan, 1989, 1st published 1965, p.292 onwards.
26. Turner, Mary, *The Woman's Century 1900–2000*, The National Archives London, 2003. p.46.
27. Pollard, Sydney, *The Development of the British Economy*, Edward Arnold, 1962, pp.77/78.
28. *Hereford Times*, I Remember, 1 January 1938.

Chapter 2 The Early History of the Site
1. Unless otherwise stated the details in this chapter can be found in Morriss, Richard K., *The Chapel of Our Lady of the Assumption, Rotherwas near Hereford. A brief guide,* privately published, date unknown.
2. Blount, Thomas, *A History of Herefordshire*, Botsum and Reeves 1985, p.55.
3. Ray, Dr. Keith, comments taken from Giffard & Partners, *Rotherwas Ordnance Factory Management Study*, Volume 1, 2001.

4. HRO BC 79/22B, *Funeral of Count Lubienski*.
5. Edwards, Russell & Baldwin, *The Rotherwas Estate*, Sale Catalogue, 1912, held at Hereford Library.
6. *Hereford Times*, various dates between October 1912 and January 1913.
7. *Kelly's Directory for Herefordshire*, 1941, accessed at the Hereford Record Office.
8. *Hereford Times*, 18 January 1913.
9. *Country Life*, 13 January 1913, accessed at Hereford Library included in the sale particulars.
10. PRO T 161/134. ANON, *Documents relating to the sale of land for National Filling Factory No. 14 Hereford*.
11. *Hereford Times*, 11 January 1913.
12. PRO MUN 5/154/1122-3/35-48.
13. Imperial War Museum, *Women at War*, Reel 74.
14. Geddes, Sir Eric (1875–1937). Little known but influential figure, originally a railway manager. Lloyd George, then the Minister of Munitions, appointed him as deputy director of supply in 1915. The next year he was given the honorary rank of Major General and headed the BEF transport section before taking over as the army's Inspector General of Transport. In May 1917 he was given the rank of Vice Admiral and became administrative controller of the Royal Navy where despite opposition from First Sea Lord Jellicoe he was instrumental in introducing the convoy system which did much to counter the success of the German U-boats. In 1918 he was elected to parliament and served in the cabinet for several years.
15. PRO MUN 5/154/1122-3/35-43.
16. Cocroft, Wayne D., *Dangerous Energy*, English Heritage, 2000, p.134.
17. *Hereford Times*, 8 January 1916.
18. PRO MUN 5/154/1122-3/35-43.
19. PRO MT 2499/9.
20. PRO MUN 5/154/1122-3/35-43.
21. PRO MUN 5/154/1122-3/44-58.
22. PRO MUN 5/154/1122-3/44-58.
23. Brown, G.I., *The Big Bang*, Sutton Publishing, 1998, p.161.
24. PRO MUN 5/154/1122/35-43 and 44-58.
25. PRO MUN 5/154/1122/35-43 and 44-58.
26. PRO *History of the Ministry of Munitions*, Vol. 7, Part 5. p.40.
27. PRO MUN 5/909.
28. HRO *Minutes of the Hereford Deanery Committee*, 7 July 1916.
29. IWM *Women at War*, op. cit., Reel 74.
30. PRO MUN 5/154/1122/35-43 and 44-58.
31. PRO MUN 5/186/86.
32. PRO MUN 5/154/1122-3/35-43.
33. PRO MUN 5/154/1122-3/44-58.
34. Survey by the author.
35. HRO G36/1/63, The Bustin Collection.
36. Field trip to Banbury NFF No. 5 on 6 February 2002.
37. PRO SUPP 5/990.
38. JE Map 2, dated 1923.
39. PRO MUN 5/154/1122-3/44-58.
40. JE Map 2, dated 1923.
41. PRO MUN 5/154/1122-3/58.
42. *Hereford Times*, 8 January 1938.
43. Buchanan, R.A., *Industrial Archaeology in Britain*, 2nd edition, Penguin, 1982, Fig.56.
44. PRO MUN 5/154/1122-3/35-43.
45. *Ibid*.
46. *Hereford Times*, 17 June 1916.
47. *Ibid*.
48. *Hereford Times*, 19 August 1916.
49. *Hereford Times*, 8 December 1917.

50. HRO L65/1 *Minutes of the Hereford Deanery Committee*, 7 July 1916.
51. IWM *Women at War., op. cit.*, Reel 74.
52. HRO G36/A/1/63 *The Wet Bar*, The Bustin collection.
53. Reports on the Guildhall Magistrates Court—*Hereford Times* & *Hereford Journal*, June 1916 onwards.
54. *Hereford Journal*, 23 September 1916.
55. Laws, Bill, *Amazing How Times Change. Hereford Remembered*, Hereford City Council, 1992.
56. IWM. *Women at War, op. cit.*, Reel 74.

Chapter 3 The Filling Operation during the First World War
1. Unless otherwise stated the information in this the Lyddite Section is taken from PRO MUN 5/186/86.
2. PRO MUN 5/186/1340/26.
3. PRO MUN 5/186/1340/25-38.
4. Unless otherwise stated the information in this the Amatol Section is taken from PRO MUN 5/186/86.
5. Brown, I.G., *The Big Bang. A History of Explosives*, Sutton Publishing, 1998, p.161.
6. Conversation with Mrs. Peggy Jones, December 2000.
7. Times, *History of the War*, Vol. XI, chapter 126. p.322.
8. PRO MUN 4/1725.
9. IWM *Women at War, op. cit.*, Reel 74.
10. Unless otherwise stated the information in this section is taken from PRO MUN 5/186/140/25-38.
11. PRO SUPP 6/622 and WO 142/274.
12. PRO SUPP 6/622.
13. PRO SUPP 6/622 and WO 142/274.
14. PRO SUPP 590.
15. Haber, L.F., *The Poisonous Cloud, op. cit.*, p.251.
16. PRO SUPP 6/622.
17. PRO SUPP 5/990.

Chapter 4 Labour in The First World War
1. Sillars, Stuart, *Women in World War 1*, Macmillan, 1987, p.106.
2. Mackenzie, Midge, *Shoulder to Shoulder*, Penguin, 1975, p.11.
3. Braydon, Gail, *Women Workers in the Fisrt World War*, Croom Helm, 1981, p.44.
4. IWM. *Women at War*, Reel 74.
5. *Ibid.*, Reel 73.
6. Collins, William, *Herefordshire in the Great War*, Jakeman & Carver, 1926, p.64.
7. PRO MUN 5/155/1122/44-58.
8. PRO SUPP 6/990.
9. Times, *History of the War*, Vol. IV., chapter 78, p.457 onwards.
10. Collins, William, *op. cit.*, p.58.
11. IWM. *Women at War, op. cit.*, Reel 73.
12. *Hereford Times*, 17 March 1917.
13. PRO MUN 5/154/1122-3/36.
14. IWM. *Women at War, op. cit.*, Reel 74.
15. Collins, William, *op. cit.*, p.87.
16. IWM. *Women at War, op. cit.*, Reel 73.
17. PRO MUN 5/154/1122-3/36.
18. PRO MUN 5/186/1340/25-38.
19. IWM. *Women at War, op. cit.*, Reel 74.
20. PRO MUN 5/155/1122-3/44-58 *Rules for Employees in Ammunition Filling Factories*.
21. *Hereford Journal*, 27 October 1917 and later editions.
22. Taylor, A.J.P., *English History 1914–1945*, Clarendon Press, 1965, p.38.
23. *Hereford Times*, 'I Remember', 2 October 1937.
24. Sillars, Stuart, *op. cit.*, p.17.
25. *Hereford Times*, 6 July 1918.

26. *Hereford Journal*, 3 March 1917.
27. *Hereford Journal*, 25 March 1917.
28. *Hereford Journal*, 14 July 1917.
29. IWM. *Women at War, op. cit.*, Reel 73.
30. *Hereford Times*, during 1918.
31. HRO *Hereford Deanery Committee*, July 1916.
32. *Hereford Times*, 20 October 1917.
33. PRO MT 6 2499/9.
34. Map drawn by R. Stamp, Swindon Loco and Carriage Department. Undated but thought to be *circa* 1918.
35. PRO SUPP 5/990.
36. Laws, Bill, (ed.), *Amazing How Times Change. Hereford Remembered*, Hereford City Council, 1992, p.9.
37. *Hereford Times*, 9 June 1917.
38. PRO MUN 5/155/1122.3/55.
39. PRO MUN 4/1725. *Report by J.B. Strain to General Millman*.
40. PRO, *History of the Ministry of Munitions*, Vol. V, Part III, unpublished, 1920, pp.73 and 74.
41. IWM. *Women at War, op. cit.*, Reel 74.
42. IWM. *Women at War, op. cit.*, Reel 75.
43. PRO, *History of the Ministry of Munitions*, Vol. V, Part III, p.71.
44. Collins, William, *op. cit.*, p.87
45. *Hereford Journal*, 24 February 1917.
46. *Hereford Journal*, 13 January 1917.
47. *Hereford Times*, 4 August 1917.
48. PRO MUN 5/15/1122-3/44-58.
49. *Hereford Times*, 20 October 1917.
50. *Hereford Times*, 4 November 1916.
51. Sparticus.schoolnet.co.uk/Wpatrols.
52. Times, *History of the War*, Vol. 17., chapter 221, p.443 onwards.
53. *The East Grinstead Reporter*, 13 November 1915.
54. De Groot, Gerald, *Blighty. British Society in the Era of the Great War*, Longman, 1996, p.62.
55. Collins, William, *op. cit.*, p.62.
56. *Hereford Journal*, 1 January 1919.
57. Collins, William, *op. cit.*, p.62.
58. *Hereford Journal*, 13 January 1917 and 24 February 1917.

Chapter 5 November 1918 to September 1939
1. IWM Women at War, *op. cit.*, Reel 73.
2. De Groot, Gerald, *op. cit.*, p.262.
3. *Hereford Times*, 16 November 1918.
4. *Hereford Times*, 23 November 1918.
5. *Hereford Times*, 30 November 1918.
6. Collins, William, *op. cit.*, p. 62.
7. *Hereford Journal*, 27 November 1920.
8. Edwards, Brian, *National Filling Factory No. 5, Quedgley, Gloucester*, private publication, date unknown.
9. Stratton, Michael & Trinder, Barrie, *Twentieth Century Industrial Archaeology*, E & FN Spoon, 2000, p.97.
10. *Hereford Times*, 19 April 1919.
11. *Hereford Times*, November 1919.
12. *Hereford Times*, 20 March 1920.
13. *Hereford Journal* & *Hereford Times*, April 1920–March 1923.
14. *Hereford Journal*, April–August 1920.
15. PRO CAB 102/625.
16. *Hereford Journal* and *Hereford Times*, 14 August 1920.
17. *Hereford Journal*, 12 March 1921.
18. PRO *History of the Ministry of Munitions*, op. cit., Vol. II, p.44.
19. *Hereford Times*, 13 January 1923.
20. *Hereford Times*, 13 & 20 January 1923.
21. *Hereford Times*, December 1926.

22. PRO CAB 102/625.
23. Taylor, A.J.P., *English History*, op. cit., p.409.
24. Conversation with Mrs. Peggy Jones, December 2000.

Chapter 6 Chemical Warfare from 1918 Onwards
1. Haber, L.F., *The Poisonous Cloud*, op. cit., p.286.
2. Carver, Field Marshall Lord, *Britain's Army in the 20th Century*, Macmillan, 1988, pb edition Pan Books, p.12.
3. PRO SUPP 6/622 *Gas Charging Reports 1 –10, No. 8 Hereford*.
4. PRO SUPP 5/590 *Royal Ordnance Factory Hereford. Gas Charging Records, 1927*.
5. PRO SUPP 5/590.
6. *Hereford Times*, 14 December 2000.
7. PRO SUPP 5/590.
8. PRO SUPP 5/590.
9. PRO CAB 102/625.
10. PRO SUPP 5/590.
11. PRO SUPP 5/590.
12. PRO T 161/875 *Notes on the UKs Policy Regarding Chemical Warfare 1920–1939*.
13. PRO T 161/875.
14. PRO *Declaration on Chemical Warfare*, p.2.
15. PRO CAB 102/625.

Chapter 7 Rotherwas at War — 1939 to 1945
1. Taylor, A.J.P., *British History*, op. cit., p.459.
2. Stratton, Michael & Trinder, Barrie, *Twentieth Century Industrial Archaeology*, op. cit, p.102.
3. Cocroft, Wayne, *Dangerous Energy*, op. cit., p.211.
4. Dewey, Peter, War and Progress. Britain 1914 –1945, Longman, 1997.
5. Murphy, Mary, *The War Economy. 1939 to 1943*, Professional and Trade Press, 1943, p.96 onwards.
6. Pollard, Sydney, *The development of the British Economy*, Edward Arnold, 1962, p.324 onwards.
7. *Ibid*.
8. Calder, Angus, *The People's War. Britain 1934 to 1945*, Cape, 1969, p.140.
9. Pollard, Sydney, op. cit., p.324 onwards.
10. *Hereford Times*, 31 August 1946.
11. Hornby, William, *Factories and Plant*, HMSO, 1958, p.99.
12. Postin, M.M., Hay, D. & Scott, J.D., *Design and Development of Weapons*, HMSO, 1960.
13. HRO 46/24 File 714.
14. *Hereford Times*, 15 July 1939.
15. *Hereford Times*, 16 December 1939.
16. Hornby, William, op. cit., p.99.
17. *Hereford Times*, 23 November 1940.
18. Inman, P., *Labour in the Munition Factories*, HMSO, 1957, p.268.
19. Hornby, William, op. cit., p.103.
20. Inman, P., op. cit., p. 268.
21. PRO DSIR 13.525 Visit of D.A. Parker of the water Pollution Branch.
22. *Hereford Times*, 13 April 1940.
23. *Hereford Times*, 8 June 1940.
24. Inman, P., op. cit., p.268.
25. HRO *Minutes of the Hereford Deanery Committee*, November 1939 to December 1940.
26. HRO BG 11/9 H/5 *Minutes of the Hereford City Air Raids Precautions Committee,* June to November 1940.
27. *Hereford Times*, 12 May 1940.
28. *Hereford Times*, September and October 1940.

29. Conversation with Mrs Peggy Jones, December 2000.
30. Conversation with Mrs Peggy Jones, December 2000.
31. *Hereford Times*, 7 January 1950.
32. Summerfield, Penny, *Women Workers in the 2nd World War*, Random Press, 1987, p.34.
33. Pollard, Sydney, *op. cit.*, pp.306 & 341.
34. HRO BG 11/9 H/5 *Minutes of the Hereford City Air Raids Precautions Committee*, 19 March & 3 December 1941.
35. HRO *Minutes of the Hereford Deanery Committee*, meetings through 1941.
36. *Hereford Times*, issues through 1941 and into 1942.
37. *Hereford Times*, 14 March 1942.
38. Harris, Sir Arthur, *Bomber Offensive*, Collins, 1947. This edition Greenhill Books, 1990. p.89.
39. Terraine, John, *The Right of the Line. The Royal Air Force in the European War 1939–1945*, Hodder & Stoughton, 1985. This edition Wordsworth Military Library, 1997, p.280.
40. Trinder, Barrie, lecture, University of Birmingham, January 1999.
41. *Hereford Times*, 6 June 1942.
42. Evans, A., *The Bombing of the Royal Ordnance Factory at Rotherwas*, author's collection.
43. Conversations with Mrs. M. Smith and Mr. Gordon Morris, May 2000.
44. Conversation with Mrs. Phyllis Taylor, March 2001.
45. HRO BK 16 *Personal Reminiscences of the Hereford Branches*, Hereford, undated.
46. Conversation with Mr. Morris, May 2000.
47. Conversation with Mrs. Margaret Smith, May 2000.
48. Telephone Conversation with Edward (surname not given), March 2000.
49. Evans, A., *op. cit.*
50. Aerial photograph, NMR Library No. 8410, Sortie No. 13N/UK795. Flight dated 22 October 1941.
51. Conversation with Mrs. Peggy Jones, December 2000.
52. Conversation with Mrs. Gittings, June 1998.
53. Evans, A., *op. cit.*
54. Conversation with Mrs. Sally Price, May 2000.
55. Conversation with Mr. Harry Malin, December 2000.
56. *Hereford Times*, October 1942.
57. *Hereford Times*, 19 December 1942.
58. HRO *Minutes of the Hereford Deanery Committee*, meetings through 1942.
59. Calder, Angus, *op. cit.*, p.117.
60. HRO BG 11/9 H/5 *Minutes of the Hereford City Air Raids Precautions Committee*, 12 May 1942.
61. Summerfield, Penny, *op. cit.*, pp.36 & 34.
62. *Hereford Times*, 25 April 1942.
63. Harry Malin, *op. cit.*
64. McCamley, N.J., *Secret Underground Cities*, Leo Cooper, 1998, p.113.
65. Aerial photograph, see note 50.
66. Wheal, E.A. & Pope, Stephen, *Macmillan Dictionary of the Second World War*, Macmillan, 1989, pb edition 1997, p.441.
67. Calder, Angus, *op. cit.*, p.115.
68. Harris, Sir Arthur, *op. cit.*, p.113.
69. Liddel Hart, Basil, *History of the Second World War*, Cassell, 1970, pb edition Papermac, 1997, p.634.
70. PRO SUPP 5/1260. Historical Notes on the Royal Ordnance Factories.
71. *Hereford Times*, 27 June 1942.
72. Summerfield, Penny, *op. cit.*, p.78.
73. Summerfield, Penny, *op. cit.*, p.125.

74. Calder, Angus, *op. cit.*, p.115.
75. Healy, Tim, *Life on the Home Front*, Readers Digest, 1993, p.42.
76. Summerfield, Penny, *op. cit.*, p.34.
77. Conversation with Mrs. Peggy Jones, December 2000.
78. McCamley, N.J., *op. cit.*, p.113.
79. HRO BG 11/9 H/5 *Minutes of the Hereford City Air Raids Precautions Committee*, 13 December 1943.
80. Terraine, John, *op. cit.*, pp.605 & 620.
81. McCamley, N.J., *op. cit.*, pp.133–134.
82. Hay, Ian, *ROF. The Story of the Royal Ordnance Factories. 1938-1948*, HMSO, 1949.
83. PRO SUPP 5/1260 & *Hereford Times*, 13 January 1945.
84. Conversation with Mrs. Carmichael, March 2000.
85. Hay, Ian, *op. cit.*
86. Conversation with an SAS officer, September 2000.
87. Map ROF H. D. No. 1 and aerial photograph NMR Library No. 427, Sortie No. 1066/UK/1652, flight dated 11 July 1946.
88. Conversation with Mrs. Lewis, May 2000.
89. HRO AW 46/256 File 78 *Claims for Damages*.
90. Conversation Mrs. E. Godding, March 2000.
91. Hay, Ian., *op. cit.*
92. Conversation with Mrs. Lewis and Mrs. Hughes, May 2000.
93. Conversation Mrs. Carmichael, March 2000.
94. Conversation with Mrs. Edwards.
95. Hay, Ian, *op. cit.*
96. *Hereford Times*, 3 June 1944.
97. Pollard, Sydney, *op. cit.*, p.308.
98. PRO SUPP 5/1260 *op. cit.*
99. *Hereford Times*, 31 December 1950.

Chapter 8 Wartime Accommodation Developments in Hereford
1. PRO DEF 51/57 *Records of the Ministry of Defence, Hereford. Procedures for the Compulsory Purchase of Land needed for the Militia Camp*.
2. Conversation with Mrs. Lewis.
3. HRO AW 46 Box 265 *ROF and the Hostel*.
4. *Hereford Times*, 31 December 1950.
5. Conversation with Mrs. Lewis.
6. Conversation with Mrs. Price.
7. PRO DEF 51/57, *op. cit.*
8. *Hereford Times*, 6 March 1948.
9. HRO AW 46 Box 265 *op. cit.*
10. Hirst, Neil, *The 50 Years of a Lighting Company in Hereford*, private publication, 1999.
11. *Hereford Times*, 6 March 1948.
12. HRO AW 46 Box 124.

Chapter 9 The Change to Civilian Use
1. Much of the information in this chapter comes from a study of the *Hereford Times* from 1945 onwards.
2. Conversation with Mrs. Taylor.
3. Halcrow plc, *Report to the Hereford Council on a Site Visit to the Rotherwas Industrial Estate*, 30 October 1998.
4. *Ibid.*
5. Conversation with Eric Gittoes, MD Artic Gold.
6. Conversation with Andrew Terry, Estates Officer, Herefordshire Council.
7. NMR Library No. 427, Sortie No. 1066/UK/1652 dated 11/7/46.
8. NMR Library No. 8410, Sortie No. 13N/UK/795 dated 22/10/41.
9. PRO DSIR. ANON *Report by the Water Pollution Laboratory on the treatment of water from Harcourts Ltd. Hereford*.

10. Hirst, Neil, *The 50 years of a Lighting Company*, *op. cit.*, p.8.
11. *Ibid.*
12. McCamley, N.J., *Secret Underground Cities*, *op. cit.*, p.135.
13. World War Railway Study Group. MoD unnumbered plan of the railway layout at Rotherwas dated by the Group as being circa 1960.
14. Comparison of the aerial photographs of 1946 and 1961.
15. Conversation with Bert Hines, ex GWR train driver, October 2000.
16. Halcrow plc., *op. cit.*
17. Conversation with Andrew Terry, Estates Officer, Herefordshire Council.
18. Halcrow plc., *op. cit.*
19. The Industrial Locomotive Society, *Industrial Locomotives of Cheshire, Shropshire and Herefordshire*.

Index

Many entries are given under the overall heading Rotherwas Royal Ordnance Factory,
whilst other munitions factories mentioned are listed under the heading Royal Ordnance Factories

Abel, Elsie Francis 44
accommodation 41, 61-62, 79-82
    billeting 41, 63, 64, 70, 71
    Bradbury Lines 79, 80
    Castle Close, Broad Street 42
    Clearing Hostel 36, 37
    Highlands Hostel, Broomy Hill 42
    Holly Mount 42
    Judge's Lodging House, Commercial Street 44
    New Womens Hostel 42
    Red Hill Hostel 65, 70, 80-1
    YWCA 42
Ainslee, Dr. William 53, 54
amatol 3,4, 13, 29, 30, 31, 50, 51, 72
ammonium nitrate 31
Ammunition Supply Depots 73
Arctic Gold 83
Aulsehurst, Winifred 50, 51

Baker, Miss Lillian *39*, 40
Baines, Frank *97*
Beakbane, C.F. 50
Biggs, H.F.B. 83
Bodenham family 9
    Sir Charles de la Barre 9, 11
    Sir Roger 9
breech loading shells 4, 23, 58
British Lighting Industries Ltd. 86
British Thompson Houston Co. Ltd. 86

'**c**anaries' 46
Carmichael, Mrs. 75

Chamney, Miss 44
Churchill, Winston 2, 49
Civil War, The 9
Committee for Chemical Warfare Research 53, 54, 55
Control of Employment Act 1939 59
Crawthorne, Mona 75, *77*
Credenhill site 16, 47, 49, 51
    explosion at 51

Defence of the Realm Act 20
depth charges 51, 52
detonators 4
Deyn Plastics 98
Dilution 35, 47, 50
Dunnett, Mr. 40
    Mrs. 40

Eastwood, Mrs. 39
Edison Swan Electric Ltd. 86
Edwards, Mrs. Ann 76
Employment (general) 7, 35-36, 46, 59, 60, 64, 71-72
    (at Rotherwas) 7,8, 20, 36-45, 62
        attitude to workers 43-45, 62, 65, 70
        Committee of Inquiry into the Shortage of Labour 38, *39*
        Rules of Employment 40
        unrest 42-43
        wages 40, 62, 67, 87
        working practices 59-60
Essential Works Order 1941 64
Evans, Mr. 67, 68
    Mrs. Doris 70

Firemen's Row 82
First World War
    Armistice 47
    artillery 1
    munitions industry 2, 3
    shell manufacture 24-34
        exploder 34
        formering 25, *27*
        grummeting 30, 34
        kitting 25, *27*
        filling *26*
        propellant charge 30
        stemming 29, *60*, 72
Fitzmaurice, Mr. W.L. 76
fuzes 4

gas, use of in war 4, 5, 11, 53-58
    at Rotherwas 28, 31-34, *32*, *33*
    chlorine 5
    mustard 6, 53
    sulphur dioxide 5
    Yperite 6
Gaudet, Col. 47
Geddes, Eric 11
Geneva Protocol 1925 53
George Cohen & Co. Ltd. 51, 87
Gibbs, James 9
Gilbert, son of Thorold 9
Greenland, Mr. 11

Hague Convention of 1907 5
Harcourt & Co. Ltd. 86
Harding, Mrs. 40
Harris, Air Marshall Sir Arthur 67
Haywood Ordnance Storage Depot 71, 72
Health of Munitions Committee 7, 39
Hereford Deanery Committee 62, 65, 70

Hereford Motor Co. 20
Hereford Pistol Club 90
Hereford Women's Patrols 44
Hildeyard, Thomas 10
Hirst, Neil 81
Hotpoint Electrical Co. Ltd. 86
Hughes, Mrs. 75
Hulbard, Mr. 63
Hursey, Ken 68
    Police Superintendent & Mrs. E.J. 68
    Corporal and Mrs. V. 68

ICI, Randle plant 55
Jones, George 51
    Mrs. Peggy 63, 68, 70
Jutland, Battle of 3

Kenchester, Pontithel Works 32
Knox-Gore, Col. 40

Lampitt, Harold 51
Levenstein, Manchester 6
Lewis, Mr. F.A. 73
    Mrs. 75
licensing restrictions 20
Little, Mr. J.W. 73
Livens Projector 5, *5*, 6
Lloyd George 2, 7, 35
Lloyd, Mrs. C.M. 72
Lotinga, Mary 43
Lubienski(-Bodenham), Count 9
lyddite 3, 4, 19, 21, 24

Mayhew, Mr. 10
Mckenna, Major 51
Milne, Mr. J.F. 16
mines 51

Moorlands Villa 68, *69*
Moreton-on-Lugg 67
Morris, Mr. A.G. 73
       Mr. G. 68
Mowlem, James & Co. Ltd. 16

National Factory 27, 30, 35, 37, 38, 47, 48

Ovens, Digby 53, 54, 65, 83

Pankhurst, Emmeline & Sylvia 7
Parsons, G.W. 64, 72
picric acid (see lyddite)
Pontithel Works, Kenchester 32
Pontrilas Developments 97, 99
       Ordnance Storage Depot 71, 83
Porton Down (Dorset) 53
Pugin, Edward 9

quick firing ammunition 4, 52, 58, *64*

railways 42, 50
       locomotives 99
RDX 61
Representation of the People Act 1918 46
Right to Serve March 1915 7
Roberts, S. (M.P.) 50
Rotherwas Chapel 9, 10, *10*, 11
       Estate 9-11, *12*
           allotments and smallholdings 10, 11
       House 9, 16, 51
           sale of contents 11
Rotherwas Royal Ordnance Factory
       administration centre 18, *97*
       air raid shelters 88-90, *88*, *89*, *90*
       ammonium nitrate stores 17, *17*, 28
           dryer 28

A.O.D. stores 13, 15, 16, 47, 100, 100, 101
blast areas 92, *92*, *93*, 94
boiler houses 18, *18*, 19, *56*, 57-58, *57*
bomb filling (First World War) 38
       (Second World War) 71, 72
bombing raid on 1942 67-70, *69*
bond stores 24, 94
breaking-down operation 83
canteen 18
clean and dirty ways 90-91, *91*
closure 83
construction workers 19-20
Decauville narrow gauge railway *15*, 25, 50
decontamination building *57*
development of 4, 7, 11-20
drainage 18
earth traverses 17, *98*
electric power 19
empty shell stores 17, 21, *22*, *23*, 96, *96*, *97*
expense stores 94, *94*, *95*
explosions at (see also bombing raid on)
       April 1920 50
       September 1940 63
       September 1941 65
       October 1942 70
       December 1942 (in railway wagon) 70
       May 1944 73-77, *74*, *76*
First World War operation 21-34
gas masks, assembly of 83, 87
gas shells 28, 31-34, *32*, **33**, 53-58, *54*, *56*, *57*
honesty boxes 97, *97*
hospital 18, 50
incorporation houses 28
       mills 29, *29*, 63, 56
melt houses 25
Northern, lyddite, Section 13, *15*, *18*, 19, 20, 24-28, *24*, *26*, *27*
output 28, 31, 34, 60, 78

picric acid expense stores *18*
pillboxes 99
private industrial use 83, 86-87
producer gas plant 19, 25
road access 100
Romney Huts 86, *100*, 101
Second World War operation 59-78
Southern, amatol, Section 13, *17*, 28-31
storage depot, use as 83
        auction sales 86
TNT expense stores 28
TNT magazines 16, 17, *17*, 28, 98, *98*, 99
transit sheds 30, 98
watchtower 99
water supply 19

Royal Ordnance factories
    Aintree (Liverpool) 38
    Ardeer (Scotland) 3
    Avonmouth 6, 34
    Banbury (Oxon) 6, 11, 18, 25, *33*, 47, 50, 53
    Bridgend (Glamorgan) 51-52, 78
    Bridgwater (Somerset) 61
    Burton-on-Trent 47
    Castle Bromwich (Warwickshire) 59
    Chillwell (Notts) 11, 13, 38
    Chittening 6, *33*
    Chorley (Lancs) 51, 62
    Coventry 49
    Georgetown (Renfrew) 38
    Glascoed (Monmouths) 52, 71, 78, 87
    Gretna 47
    Hayes (Middlesex) 38
    Morecombe (Lancs) 11
    Oldbury (West Midlands) 3
    Penrhyndeudraeth (Gwynedd) 3
    Perivale (Middlesex) 38, 49
    Quedgley (Glos) 38, 42, 47
    Slough 2, 49
    Sutton Oak (Lancs) 55
    Woolwich 30, *39*, 47, 50, 51, 52, 62

St. Charles House, Lower Bullingham 10
St. George's Garage, Eign Street 20
Sankey & Sons Ltd. 86
Second World War
        development of munitions 61, 67
sewage works 18, 87
shadow factories 59
Sigeric 9
Smith, Mrs. Margaret 68
Stokes, Mr. 30

Taylor, Mr. E.A. 11
       Mrs. 67
Thomas, Mr. Edward 77
Thorn Lighting Ltd. 86, *97*
TNT 3, 13, 28, 30, 31, 34, 43, 72
    poisoning 7, *29*, 71
torpedoes 51, 52
Toxic Jaundice (see TNT, poisoning)
Tranter, Annie 50
Tyler, Mr. F.J. 73

Vincent, Major 47

Warter, Philip 83
welfare 7, 39
Weston, Mr. 63, 64
Whitham, G.S. 55
Wit, Mrs. H.E. 65
Women Police Services 44
        Volunteers 44
Wood, Sir Kingsley 59